CANDLE MAKING FOR BEGINNERS

The definitive step by step guide to creating incredible homemade candles with different fragrances, essential oils, herbs, spices and colors.

ELLA DIAMOND

Contents

HISTORY ABOUT CANDLE MAKING 1

CHAPTER ONE 9

    An Introduction to Candle Making..9

    The Different Types of Candles...12

    Candle Making Tips to Make the Most Beautiful Candles!13

    How to Make Grunge Candles 18

CHAPTER TWO 22

    What are Molds for Candles?...22

    Candle Making Molds..25

    Use Candle Making Molds To Make Unique Candles.........26

    Which Molds For Candles Are Right For You? 30

    How to Effectively Clean Your Candle Molds 30

CHAPTER THREE 33

    Basics of All Candle Making Recipes......................................33

    Candle Making Recipes Used For Fancy Candles 36

    Candle Types and Candle Making Tips..................................39

    Tips in Candle Making 41

    Safety Tips on Candle Making 42

CHAPTER FOUR 44

    Making Candle Wicks for Candle Making 44

    Candle Making and Interior Design..47

    Soy Scented Candles 49

    Reasons Why Scented Candles Have Become So Popular 52

    Tips on How to Make Your Own Scented Candles 56

    Soy Candle Making 59

    The Health Benefits Of Soy Candle Making........................61

    Quality Candle Making Scents Make Better Candles..........63

    The benefits of choosing better quality candle making scents 64

    How to Choose Your Candle Making Wax...........................66

CHAPTER FIVE 69

Candle Making Business 69
Make Unique Candles At Home 71
Candle Making Crafts for Any Holiday or Special 75
Why You Should Absolutely Learn Candle Making 77

CHAPTER SIX 83

Candle Making Wax 83
Why You Should Choose All-Natural Candles 87

CHAPTER SEVEN 90

Reasons To Make Your Own Homemade Candles 90
Benefits of Making Candles Instead of Buying 93
Reasons Why Every Home Should Have Candles 94
Candle Making as Therapy 96

CHAPTER EIGHT 98

Ways to Use Candles 98
Using Candles As Garden Lights 101
Use Candles in a Wedding Ceremony 103
Use Candles to Spice Up a Night at Home 105
Decorate Your Home for Valentine's Day Candles 107
Things To Think About When Using Candle Lighting ... 109
Using Candles As Fireplace Decorations 110
How to Make Candles in a Variety of Designs 112
Stamps 113
Stencils 113
Wax 114

CHAPTER NINE 115

Candle Making Equipment 115
Basics 119
Extra 120
Candle Making Supplies Tips and Tricks 122

CHAPTER TEN **125**

    Making Your Own Wicks 125
    Everything You Need to Know 125
    Types of Wicks 127
    Which Wicks to Use When Making Candles..................... 129
    How to Choose a Candle Wick 132
    What's the Best Type of Candle?........................ 134

CHAPTER ELEVEN **138**

    Step by Step Melting Wax Candle Making........................ 138
    Basic Component of Any Candle........................ 140
    Making Gel Candles for Fun & Profit................ 143
    Dyes & Scents:... 144
    Heating Wax:.. 145
    CAUTION: 145
    Clean Up: 145

CONCLUSION **146**
DISCLAIMER **147**

**© Copyright 2019 by Ella Diamond
All rights reserved.**

This document is geared towards providing exact and reliable information with regards to the topic and issue covered. The publication is sold with the idea that the publisher is not required to render accounting, officially permitted, or otherwise, qualified services. If advice is necessary, legal or professional, a practiced individual in the profession should be ordered.

- From a Declaration of Principles which was accepted and approved equally by a Committee of the American Bar Association and a Committee of Publishers and Associations.

In no way is it legal to reproduce, duplicate, or transmit any part of this document in either electronic means or in printed format. Recording of this publication is strictly prohibited and any storage of this document is not allowed unless with written permission from the publisher. All rights reserved.

The information provided herein is stated to be truthful and consistent, in that any liability, in terms of inattention or otherwise, by any usage or abuse of any policies, processes, or directions contained within is the solitary and utter responsibility of the recipient reader. Under no circumstances will any legal responsibility or blame be held against the publisher for any reparation, damages, or monetary loss due to the information herein, either directly or indirectly.

Respective authors own all copyrights not held by the publisher.

The information herein is offered for informational purposes solely, and is universal as so. The presentation of the information is without contract or any type of guarantee assurance.

The trademarks that are used are without any consent, and the publication of the trademark is without permission or backing by the trademark owner. All trademarks and brands within this book are for clarifying purposes only and are the owned by the owners themselves, not affiliated with this document

HISTORY ABOUT CANDLE MAKING

Flip a switch and turn on a light! If there is one thing about modern life we really take for granted, it is indoor electric lighting. Imagine, if you will, a home in the Middle Ages. It is night, and the day's hard work is done. A single candle lights the interior of the room. This candle provides light for the family's night time activities. It occupies a distinguished position in human history. The candle is one of mankind's earliest inventions. The history of candle making is a long and interesting story.

The candle uses wax as fuel to produce light. Once the wick of a candle is lighted, heat from the flame burns the wax, which flows into the wick by capillary action. It's a simple device, and it ruled the night for thousands of years.

Archeological digs have unearthed candlesticks in Egyptian and Cretan sites dating to about 3000 BC. Before this the Egyptians used a device called a rush light. A rush light was made from the pithy core of the rush plant, which was soaked in tallow and burned for light.

Tallow was the main ingredient of candles for thousands of years. Tallow is processed from the fat of cattle and sheep. These candles emit a very disagreeable odor and a lot of smoke when burned. They were used to light homes, temples, and meeting places. Travelers used them to light their way.

It is the Romans who probably learned how to make candles from beeswax. Beeswax is superior to tallow because it burns much cleaner, and is odorless. But it was also very expensive, so its use was limited to the nobility and the Church.

American Colonial women discovered that a superior wax could be extracted from the bayberry. This wax was very clean burning and produced a sweet aroma. The difficulty in extracting the wax from the berry prevented it from replacing the more readily available tallow.

Whales have the bad fortune to have a substance called spermaceti in their enormous bodies. Spermaceti produces a very high quality wax which makes candles superior to both tallow and beeswax. Since it is harder than these other waxes, the candles don't bend in hot weather, a common problem for tallow and beeswax candles. By the 1700's the whaling industry was supplying this highly valued substance for use. Candle making has always been a labor intensive business. Wax has to be melted and hand poured into molds. Taper candles, the earliest candles made, must be dipped many times to make a candle. Molded candle production became a lot easier in 1834 because of a gentleman by the name of Joseph

History About Candle Making

Morgan. Mr. Morgan invented a candle molding machine. This machine consisted of a mold which had a moveable cylinder for its bottom. Wax was poured into the mold and allowed to cool. The cylinder bottom was then moved up, forcing the hardened wax candles out of the top. Continuous production of candles was now possible.

The best material for making candles was developed near the end of the candles long reign. Automobiles were becoming popular in the late 1800's, and the need for petroleum to fuel the new internal combustion engine became great. The leftover residues of petroleum production produced a substance called paraffin. It was ideal for the production of candles, as it was economical, clean burning, and odorless. It's chief drawback was its low melting point, which would have caused problems in warm weather. The independent discovery of stearic acid solved this problem. Added to paraffin, it hardened the candle, and slowed its burn rate. Paraffin/stearine candles soon became standard, totally replacing the tallow candle.

Thomas Edison's creation of the light bulb in 1879 ended our dependency on the candle as a light source. The candle soon passed from necessity to ornamental. Candles are still used as ceremonial and decorative lights. Skilled crafts people still make candles to light and perfume our homes.

Candle Making For Beginners

Candle making has been an essential craft in our history. Candles lit our ancestors homes and provided light for sacred ceremonies. Their manufacture contributed to the economy of the civilizations they illuminated. Today, candle making is a craft practiced by many artisans providing a link to our distant past.

Since primitive times, candle making has been considered an art form. However, as the technique became more modern a difference in designs started to appear. During primitive times, candles were necessary to provide light and heat. Today, candles provide us with decorations and a wonderful scent in our home for dinners or baths.

It is unknown when candles were first used. Clay candle holder remnants have been found at digs as far back as 4 BC, which provides us with proof that they have been around for a long time. The oldest clay candle holders were found at digs in Egypt.

During ancient times, candles were used in both Japan and China. Early candles were made from wax that came from seeds or insects. Taper candles in India came from wax extracted from boiled cinnamon. The earliest known in America came from 1 AD.

Historians believe Native American's burned oily fish and the backs of Cerio trees. Settlers from New England used very similar techniques in order to get wax from bayberries. Today, modern candle makers

History About Candle Making

use a process that is very similar in order to create bayberry candles. However, this traditional process can be very expensive.

In the 1600s and 1700s, tallow was first used as the product to make candles. Tallow is a byproduct that comes from animal fat. While tallow was effective, it also had a foul odor, especially when burned. Both beeswax and paraffin were introduced during the 1800s and tallow was discontinued.

Taper candles made from the dipping process started in 13 AD. Traveler merchants moved from town to town and made taper candles in the homes of individuals. In 15 AD, the idea for molds in the candle making process was started in Paris. Molds helped improve the candle making process, but there were still issues in getting candles to burn right.

Candle makers in the 1800s theorized that the wick was the weakest area of the candle and responsible for defective burning patterns. In 1825, a braided wick was developed that dramatically improved the burning of several different candle types. In 1830, a specific process was designed to make paraffin wax and molds. These candles not only burned well, but they were also of very good quality.

Even when electricity and gas started being used, the candle making process continued to see evolutions. Melting paraffin wax became faster and easier. Traditional elements such as the hand dipping process have stuck around largely because the popularity of candles has decreased due to the introduction of electricity.

Candle making today has become an art form. Many companies are focused on creating wonderful candles with a variety of unique fragrances. Many small businesses still focus on making candles from the home kitchen. Today, candle making is more than a business; it can also be a wonderful hobby and enjoyable activity for the entire family.

Instead of using candles for light and heat, candles are now used as a luxury and pleasure. As the candle industry expands new candle types are being introduced. The number of colors, fragrances and types of candles to choose from is stunning.

Candles are becoming a very popular option for decorating the home. You can use them to accent any room. Often they perform an excellent centerpiece for dinners or other formal occasions. In American culture, there is a deep sense of tradition in the unity candles that are used at weddings.

Candle crafting is an art form that has drastically changed throughout the years. If you are interested in trying to make your own, it is a fairly easy process. It is best to start with a container candle or a votive in order to get used to the making process. You can find a wide variety of candle making kits at a low price or books that can provide you with tips and assistance throughout the process.

How many times have you lit a candle and wondered about how it all began? Is it down to one culture and country? The answer is that any written history of the candle making of today and back into the past has to include many countries and cultures.

As far back as 3000BC we know the Egyptians were making candles out of beeswax, a type of candle that is still popular today. Around 200BC the Chinese used whale fat for their candles and, as we are too well aware, whales continued to provide blubber and oil for lamps until they have become an endangered species.

Middle Age Europe saw tallow candles grow in popularity. Tallow, which is fat from cows or sheep, became the standard material used in candles and The Tallow Chandlers Company of London was formed in about 1300. By 1415, tallow candles were used in street lighting. However the glycerine in tallow candle produced an unpleasant smell and hence beeswax candles were used for churches and royal events. If tallow candles were so unpleasant to burn, just imagine how unpleasant the smell must have been during manufacture! It was so unpleasant that the processing of fat to produce tallow for candles was banned in many areas.

American colonists made candles from bayberries but the yield was very poor. It is said that it takes about 15 pounds of bayberries to make just one pound of bayberry wax. Bayberry wax is also known as bayberry tallow or myrtle wax and is the rarest of all candle waxes. Bayberry wax has an earthy fragrance and dries to an olive green colour.

Around 1750, very expensive candles were being produced from spermaceti, found in the the head cavity of the sperm whale. Clearly cheaper alternatives were required and by 1800 an alternative was indeed discovered. Derived from plant material, the candles produced clear, smokeless flames. A further breakthrough in 1811 by French chemists saw the production of stearin, like tallow derived from animals but with no glycerine content.

CHAPTER ONE

An Introduction to Candle Making

Candle making is a creative art that involves the implementation of imagination and ideas, and it's also a lot of fun! It is a craft that has ancient and worldwide roots; this craft grew out of the need for light when the evening arrived. It is still alive today, and with a few supplies in your kit you can make your own candles. And best of all, it is not difficult for a beginner to learn.

Candles are beautiful and elegant and the demand for them is growing by consumers who want to learn how to make them. They can be tinted or colored with food coloring, crayon bits, or candle coloring (available at craft stores).

Soy candle making is now becoming increasingly popular all around the world. Soy wax candles produce less soot; in fact they produce approximately 90% less soot than paraffin candles. Soy making requires some basic ingredients, such as suitable containers, a wick, and a mason jar, but the steps themselves are easy. The number of people using soy candles is on the rise, and so is the number of stores (including supermarkets) that sell them.

Making candles is actually one of the best work-at-home opportunities available right now. It is much like cooking in that most wax formulas have a fair tolerance for inaccurate measurements. It's not difficult and with each candle you make you will find you are getting better and better. Candle making is a highly versatile craft -- one that encompasses unlimited opportunities for creativity.

Homemade candle making has has recently become a big trend. More people everyday are using candle making as a hobby and business opportunity. It's a great method to obtain meaningful presents for relatives and loved ones and also to bring in a few extra dollars if you sell them. But the art of candle making is anything but new. Long before lamps and light bulbs were even thought of, candles lit the world.

Whether you're making candles as gifts, or looking to make some cash off the craft, you must first perfect the art of candle making. You should make sure to buy high quality materials for making your candles. Molds, wicks, scents and coloring, made specifically for candle making, are available in crafts shops and online.

The first step in candle making is to melt the wax. To do this you use a double boiler. To set up your double boiler, you take a large pot and fill it with water, then place a smaller pot with the wax in it inside the bigger pot. Wax burns easily during the process of melting,

Chapter 1 : An Introduction to Candle Making

so by using a thermometer to regulate the temperature of the wax and a double boiler you reduce the risk of burning.

Place your wick carefully in the mold you chose and coat the inside of the mold with a non-stick spray to facilitate an easier removal of the finished candle. Then pour your melted wax into your mold. You can leave it to sit until the candle has solidified or you can speed the process up by placing the mold in your freezer for 30 minutes or so. When the candle has hardened completely, remove it from the mold.

There's literally no limit to the various kinds of candles available for creation in your home. With all the variations of colors, fragrances, and decorations the sky is the limit. Some candle makers have even created original latex molds to create truly spectacular looking candles.

Latex molds are very flimsy, however. It's quite difficult to fill a latex mold if you do not have something to stabilize the mold. Luckily, all you need is a simple sturdy piece of cardboard to support a latex mold. Just cut a hole large enough for the mold into the cardboard and then place the mold up to it's outward lip in the hole. You can now fill the mold with no problems.

Perfecting candle making techniques usually takes a couple of attempts, but once you've got it down, you'll be amazed by the gorgeous candles you've made and can now give away as gifts or sell with a little bit of decorative packaging.

The Different Types of Candles

Candles have always existed, and have been through the changes that man has time and again brought about. From being a travelers guide and a mode of illumination in the past, candles have today become the important and must-haves for every occasion. They have also undergone physical changes to become decorative too. Creating the ambience for any special occasion today we have numerous varieties of available on the market. Some of them are as follows.

Dinner candles

whether at hotels or homes or private parties, they are used on dinner table to create the ambience of love. There are fixed on candle holder.

Floating candles

the shape of these candles are such that buoyancy is easy. Lit and placed on water these float adding the perfect effect needed to any corner of the room. These come in various colors making them truly attractive. These days the floating candles are also scented, so that these release fragrance on being burnt.

Pillar shaped candles

as the name suggests these resemble a pillar, and are cylindrical in shape. With thick base, you need a wide base or holder. Besides, these are long-lasting too.

Gel candles

made of mineral oil or synthetic hydro carbons, they are transparent retain the shaper of the container it is poured into.

Fragrance candles

soothing in effect releasing the fragrance and aroma, they come in various different aromas. Famously used in aromatherapy, these also come in various shapes, and colors and sizes.

Wick-less candles

the wick-less candles are the modern contemporary version of them that offer radiance with fragrance when illuminated. Yes, these are illuminated indirectly by switching on the low watt bulb placed inside the candle warmer that indirectly melts the candles to emanate the perfume, and also glow to give light.

Candle Making Tips to Make the Most Beautiful Candles!

Candle Making For Beginners

There are several types of candles which are available. In fact if one does not want to buy them, they have an option of making them at home as well. The best part is that the materials are extremely easily available and the process is very simple too. There is a wide array of candles which one can make. All one needs to do is follow some simple candle making tips and steps along with a dash of creativity.

The first type of candles which one can try their hand at are gel candles. It consists of certain gelled mineral oils. The appearance of these candles are transparent and they look and feel very soft. Gel candles are usually placed inside a container. Apart from that there are container candles also which is a good option. Usually the latter is poured into a container like glass or heat which is heat resistant. One can burn the wick of the candle when one wants to use the candle.

Pillar candles are a variety that can be put into any kind of mold. After the formation of the candle, it is extracted from the container or mold. Usually the diameter can range from two to three inches with a single or multiple standing wicks. Votive candles are another attractive lot which are usually cylindrical and small. The diameter is usually 1 to 2 inches while the height is almost around 2.5 inches. The candle needs to be placed inside the votive candle holder for retention of the wax. This is undertaken for the liquefaction on lighting the candle.

Chapter 1 : An Introduction to Candle Making

One of the most common types of candle variety is taper candles. Thinner on the body, narrow at the top and wider along the base area are its main characteristics. The length is almost around six to eighteen inches in height and thus they are best utilized in a candle holder. Dinner candles are an alternative name for them.

Tea light candles are a popularly used candle for decoration and are small and cylindrical in size and shape. It is filled in a metal or plastic cup. While the diameter is approximately one to inches, the height is around 1- 1.5 inches. Floating candles is also a variety which is used for enhancing a bowl of water. The wax is poured into a mold which can be of any shape. The floating nature of these candles adds an elegant look.

Wick-less candles as the name suggests is without a wick. It is usually placed on top of a former, while the scent is emitted out of the same without a flame. It is normally poured into a heat resistant container.

These various types of candles can easily be made when one follows the below mentioned candle making tips. Some of them include the following:

The length and size of the wick is a function of the type of candle which one plans to make. Interestingly it has been noticed that the candle usually tends to melt faster with a larger wick. On the other hand the size of the wick should be in proportion to the size of the candle. In case of positioning of the wick, one

Candle Making For Beginners

would need to work with an approximate size initially. This is in accordance to the planned size of the diameter. Ensure that you use wicks which possibly have larger diameters and might not melt easily. Beeswax and paraffin wax are good examples. If you wish to have a straight candle in the central point of the candle, it is recommended that one can tie the end onto a stick which can be placed over the mold or container. In the event of using wax dye or color for the candles, one should avoid the colors which are utilized for soap or cosmetics. It leads to clogging of the wick. Use of concentrated solid or liquid colors is a good option. In the event of coloring melted wax, one should ascertain that the candle wax is basically opaque

Wicks are the most important part of any candle that you make. Without a wick, all you'd have is a big block of wax. While most people do purchase their wicks from wholesalers, it is important to know how to make your own wicks for a number of reasons. Probably the most important reason is because if you are familiar with making candle wicks, then you will also know how to deal with a problem with a wick that you've purchased, such as improper priming. So let's get started.

There are three different types of candle wicks, and each type is used for a different application.

Cored Wicks- These wicks are a basic braid with a

wire in the middle. The wire helps the wick burn hotter which is helpful for larger candles. However, recent studies have indicated that these types of candle wicks can be harmful, especially for children, because they can also release toxic metal into the air. If you are making candle wicks like this, be very careful about the wire you select.

Flat Braid Wicks- These wicks are just a basic braid. This type of wick is used for taper candles. Making candle wicks like these is a great place to start if you are a beginner because they are easy to make.

Square Braid Wicks- These wicks are a used for making any candle that is a large block of wax, such as pillar candles. Making candle wicks of this type is more difficult because the braid is more complicated.

There are two steps involved in making wicks. The first is braiding. Braiding candle wicks can be a little time consuming depending on how much you are braiding at a time. Since they are so narrow, making candle wicks in very long lengths can become tedious.

When making candle wicks, you should cut the string you are working with about six inches longer than what you want your finished candle to be. Simply soak cotton string of your desired length in a solution of 1 tablespoon of salt, 2 tablespoons of boric acid and a cup of water. Soak them in the solution for at least 12 hours (longer won't hurt them) and then hang them to dry. Once dry simply braid the strands of the string

Candle Making For Beginners

into the type of wick you want.

The second step in making candle wicks is priming. This step is crucial to your wick burning properly. All you do is saturate the wicks in wax. You just need to melt some wax and drop the wicks in. You'll know they are saturated when you see bubbles being released. At this point remove them from the wax, being careful not to burn yourself. You'll need to stretch them out tightly and dip them in water to harden the wax. Then you can lay them on a sheet of wax paper and let them dry. For a stiffer wick, allow the wick to dry for at least a minute and then repeat the process. Be sure to store your wicks properly.

How to Make Grunge Candles

Grungy candles are an easy and fast DIY candle to add to your home decor. All it takes is 15 minutes from having a pillar in your hand to the finished project and it is cheap to boot. You can find the materials right in your kitchen, garden and craft area. You don't need to be a candle maker to make and enjoy your own grungy candle.

Here is a little lesson on why primitive and grungy go hand-n-hand.

The word grungy is a slang term for soiled, dingy, grimy and grubby. It is used to describe dirty conditions or characteristics of fashion. Grungy is

Chapter 1 : An Introduction to Candle Making

associated with primitive decor because of its simple, rustic looking style.

Primitive means original, characteristic of an early stage of development, and self-taught artist.

When you make grungy candles do you think of the early stage of development of candle making and natural elements? I think of a simpler time that uses a lot of creativity to decorate the home. When I create grungy candles I think of candles with a down to earth, homey touch.

Materials Needed:

- Candle wax or an already made pillar candle
- Pillar silicone mold - if you don't have a pillar candle
- Modge Podge
- Spices, herbs, grated lemon or orange peel
- Fragrance Oil According to the spice used- if you are making your own candle
- Paint brush
- Wax paper
- Wick
- Wick pin

Directions: *Note - These directions take you from making your own pillar candle

Candle Making For Beginners

- Melt the wax and pour it into a silicone pillar mold

- Take the wick pin and place it into the center of the mold

- Secure the wick pin with 2 tightly bound bamboo skewers

- Take the pillar out of the mold, take the wick pin out of the center of the pillar and insert the wick into the hole

- Place the wax paper on a cookie tray

- Add or mix spices on the wax paper

- Take the modge podge, dip the paint brush into it and paint a strip down one side of the pillar candle

- Roll or sprinkle the spices on that strip of modge podge

- Then paint another strip down the candle and add or roll spices on that strip

- Continue with the above method until the pillar is completely covered with spices

- Seal the spices to the candle by either applying more modge podge or spraying the pillar with a matte finish sealer

- Let the pillar candle dry for 48 hours

- If you have any left over wax, melt the wax and drizzle it over the candle. It will give a

Chapter 1 : An Introduction to Candle Making

nice wax dripped look to the sides.

Warning - this is not a candle to burn. If you decide to sell these grunge candles or give them away make sure you place on these candles with a "no burn" warning label.

Add some dried apples and oranges, rosehips and dried herbs to a wooden bowl. Set your new grungy, primitive candle inside. Voila! Instant primitive decor for your home.

CHAPTER TWO

What are Molds for Candles?

Molds for candles are simply the containers used for pouring melted wax into so they will cool and form a candle in the shape of the mold. Candle making molds can be bought or made from a number of materials and in almost any shape and size.

Aluminium Candle Molds

Aluminium candle making molds are a very popular mold used by candle makers. They are popular because they have some great qualities:

They are very durable and heat resistant

They leave a very nice smooth finish and no seam in the candles finish

Give the appearance of a professionally made candle

Very popular for making pillar and votive style candles

Inexpensive compared with rubber molds

Easy to clean - just turn mold upside down in your oven and heat to 150 degrees. Place a baking sheet

Chapter 2 : What are Molds for Candles?

under the mold and the wax will run onto the baking sheet and can then be discarded.

There are a couple of down sides to aluminium candle molds though:

They are not flexible, so you are limited in the shape and texture you can give to the candle

You will need to use a releasing agent in order to get the candle out from the mold

Rubber Candle Molds

There are a few types of rubber molds for candles, like polyurethane, latex and silicone. Unlike aluminium, they are of course all very flexible, but still have their pros and cons.

Polyurethane Candle Molds

Flexible but don't stretch well

Cheaper than silicone molds

Popular for pillar and taper candles

Have a strong odor which may pass into the candle wax

Need to use a releasing agent to get the candle out from it

Latex Candle Molds

Excellent and very popular for creating your own molds using liquid latex

Losing popularity now with improvements being made in other types of rubber molds

Silicone Candle Molds

Flexible and stretchable

Easy to remove candles so no releasing agent is required

Leaves no parting lines on the candles surface

The most expensive of the rubber molds due to its excellent qualities

Plastic Candle Molds

Plastic molds are the cheapest but not usually the best choice. They are brittle and don't last as long as other types of molds for candles.

Plastic molds are easy to clean as well, just use warm soapy water. Be careful that they are completely dry before re-using though or you will end up with water bubbles in your candles.

Although plastic molds for candles are good for beginners, once you gain some expertise and want to go to the next level you will be wanting to use better alternatives for your candle making molds.

Candle Making Molds

If you've been making only container or hand dipped candles, you may not have any experience with candle making molds. Your skills as a candle maker will never be complete without learning this aspect of the candle making business.

If you aren't sure that you will continue to use molds in candle making after your initial attempt, don't spend a lot of money purchasing them in the beginning. Make a determination as to what size you would like to begin with and only purchase that size. Prices for molds vary depending on the source. Small votive molds can be purchased by the dozen for around $10. Large round molds 10 inches high cost in the neighborhood of about $12 each.

If you are planning to produce large diameter candles, it will be necessary to have more than one wick. For that reason, you may prefer to stick with molds with a 2 inch diameter or less.

Seamless molds yield prettier candles than seamed ones for obvious reasons. They may cost more than other mold types, but it's worth the expense if you are planning to sell your candles and desire a more polished professional appearance.

Molds for Cheap or Better Yet, Free

If you don't want to spend any money on candle molds, you can use other things for molds, such as tin cans. As long as the can is smooth on the inside so the candle can easily slide out, these tin molds work fine. Keep in mind if the can has a rim at the top, it will restrict the candle from easy release. Be selective in the tin cans you choose for molds.

There are a great many different kinds of molds you may choose from. Besides round and square molds, there are octagons, stars, and many other shapes. The vast majority of molds for tower candles are constructed of metal alloys; however, there are some plastic molds that are suitable for the job as well.

Use Candle Making Molds To Make Unique Candles

Many candle makers have the erroneous belief that they can just sell popular candles in a jar. While it is true that you may make a little money doing this, you should realize that you will make far more by selling unique candles. In order to do this, you will need to look into different candle making molds. In this way you will be able to make different shapes and sizes which will appeal to your customers.

Aluminum:

Chapter 2 : What are Molds for Candles?

These molds are light and easy to handle. Because they have no seams, the candle will come out smooth and perfect. Aluminum molds come in many different sizes and shapes. One of the major advantages of these molds is that they are heat resistant. You can experiment with different pouring temperatures to produce varieties of textures. This will make some very unique candles. These types of molds are good for producing pillar and votive candles.

Polyurethane:

These molds will produce seams in the candles that your make. To smooth these out, you can use a little petrolatum jelly and rub it on the seam. This will make your candle more professional looking. You should be aware that these molds have limited stretching, so you should consider using a releasing agent, such as cooking oil spray, on the mold before pouring in the wax to make it easier to remove the candle later. Sometimes you may find a strong smell from these molds which may affect your scented candles. If this is the case, you can use the more expensive silicone molds. The polyurethane molds are used for pillar and taper candles.

Latex molds:

Latex molds are not used as much as they used to be, but they do have a distinct advantage not found anywhere else. You can make your own molds from

Candle Making For Beginners

latex and increase your sales because your candles will be completely unique. You can make your candles into all sorts of unique shapes and styles, you are only limited by your imagination.

Plastic:

Plastic molds are the cheapest and most common type, which makes them ideal for beginners. They are also useful when you are experimenting with different shapes and styles of candles. Unfortunately, they do not last long because they are quite brittle and need to be handled with care. They can be cleaned with hot soapy water. However, you must be sure that the mold is completely dry before reusing, or you may get bubble marks on your candles.

With all the different molds available, you will be able to have fun experimenting and making some unique styles of candles. This will allow you to get the edge on your competitors and increase your profits. When you use candle making molds you can also use more than one color of wax, just tip the mold while it is cooling to produce some unique color effects.

Tip for Candle Release

Removing candles from molds after they set is sometimes difficult. If you do not coat the inside of the mold prior to pouring with an easy release spray, you will more than likely have problems. Using a

Chapter 2 : What are Molds for Candles?

silicone spray or wiping the inside with vegetable oil aids in the release of the finished candle. Another reason that candles stick is because the wax is too hot when it is poured into the mold. Always check the temperature of the wax before you pour for this reason.

If you do experience a problem with candle release, one tip many chandlers use is to place the mold in the freezer for a short time. Another alternative is to place the candle in a bucket as soon as it is poured and pour cool water around it. If you try this, weight the candle down so it won't float, and do not pour the water above the top of the mold.

Candle Making Kits

If you are new to the fantastic world of candle making, you could start out with a kit for making candles, complete with molds. You need to be careful to get the kit with the size and shape of a candle you may want to make. Many inexpensive kits do come with the plastic candle molds, but even these can work out if you just want to try it.

Add Variety To Your Candle Making

Tower or pillar candles look very professional when they are made correctly. If you have only made container candles, you owe it to yourself to try your hand producing a wider candle variety with candle making molds. Start out with just a few additions in the beginning. If you like the candles you produce using this method, you can add more molds to your collection a few at a time.

Which Molds For Candles Are Right For You?

Molds for candles are of course one of the essential items needed for making candles and now with the huge popularity of candle making at home by hobbyists of all kinds, it's no surprise that the variety of different candle making molds available is almost endless.

How to Effectively Clean Your Candle Molds

After every candle making project, you'll probably have to face what some think as a "less fun" part of the process - cleaning up the candle molds. Everything about candle making requires a system to make everything efficient - so even the cleaning method requires a technique to make it less daunting.

Here I'll discuss a practical, step-by-step guide that you can keep handy for your next post-project cleaning. It's actually less daunting that you think.

Your easiest choice when it comes to cleaning your candle molds would be to use a commercial cleaning

Chapter 2 : What are Molds for Candles?

kit. You can find such kits in your local hobby or crafts stores. Don't limit yourself to brick-and-mortar stores though - you can also find online stores catering to the continental US and beyond.

After you finish with making your candles, remove any leftover wax from the molds and set it aside on a neat pile. The hardened wax can be reused in your next project - you just have to melt it again. Separate scented wax from the unscented pile. Colored wax must also be separated from the neutral wax.

Remember to dispose of all excess wax properly.

Never pour the wax (whatever type of wax you are using) down the drain of your sink. If you do, the hot liquid wax will harden inside your pipes in a matter of seconds and clog your plumbing.

You can store excess wax in any container that has been lined with wax paper. The wax paper will prevent the wax from sticking to the surface of the container.

An easy way to remove wax from molds and other tools you use in your candle making project is by boiling your containers and tools. Use a large pot to do this. Fill the pot with water and bring the water to a rolling boil.

Place your candle making equipment in the water and allow the wax to melt and slough off. When the

Candle Making For Beginners

surface of your equipments is clear of wax, remove them from the boiling water with a pair tongs. Use paper towels to dry them and store them properly for your next project.

If you are washing a bunch of candle molds, you can boil them for fifteen minutes in a small pot. You can add a few drops of dishwashing liquid to the water to remove any impurities. When the wax and dirt have been removed, simply place the molds on cookie sheets.

Pre-heat your over to 190 degrees Fahrenheit. Place the molds inside the oven and allow the wax to melt for another 5 minutes. The melted wax will be absorbed by the cookie sheets. If you are using metal molds, use cleaning kits designed for metal molds.

CHAPTER THREE

Basics of All Candle Making Recipes

Candle making recipes are very similar in that they all require basically the same materials and use the same techniques. However if you are just starting out you may not know all your options that you have when making candles. Obviously, beginner candle makers don't need all the advanced ingredients that are used in many of the more elaborate candle making recipes. It is the purpose of this short article to give the basic ingredients in many candle recipes.

Beginner candle makers only need wax, wicks, candle holders and a means to melt the wax. Pretty simple. To make your most basic candle you simply melt the wax, put a wick in a holder and pour the wax in it. Let it cool and harden and you are all done.

Now what wax do you use? Most beginners start out with paraffin wax. It is cheap, popular, plentiful and easy to get. Other waxes offer other benefits. Some people like all natural products. Soy fits this category

Soy candles have been emerging as a viable alternative to the standard wax choices. Soy candles are made out of 100% natural soy wax without any additives. Candles made of soy wax will have a wonderful aroma without having to add any type of fragrance. Experienced soy candle makers can mix the soy wax in several ways that will give the natural scent a bit of a difference thus giving the scent a fainter or more powerful aroma.

Beeswax is another popular candle making wax. While it may be a little more expensive, it offers many wonder benefits. It has a natural sweet aroma, a beautiful natural color, and burns, brighter, longer and cleaner than many other candles.

Since beeswax is naturally fragrant and has a very pleasant color, no dyes or fragrances need to be added to it. However, if you were to buy beeswax sheets and roll your own candles, you could purchase these sheets in many different colors.

The last type of wax that you can use is gel wax. These are the candles that you see that have a seascape or other design in it. Gel waxes can be colored and made aromatic by adding fragrance oils.

To make candles you need wicks. Candle wicks come in many materials and can be purchased with tabs on the end so they are easier to use when making candles. When buying a wick you need something that will burn cleanly. Many people prefer cotton or hemp wicks. Others say that the wick material is dependent on the type of wax you will be using.

The last item needed to make candles is a candle

Chapter 3 : Basics of All Candle Making Recipes

holder. After you have the wax, wick and candle holder, you have all the essentials of the basic candle recipe. Molds can be purchased or you can use something around the house. Many people use glass containers that are saved or purchased solely for candle making. If you use these, you are doing it at your own risk.

Candleholder suppliers sell glass containers for candles. The reputable dealers will only sell glass candle holders that meet strict government requirements. These containers are made to be used with candles and hot wax and can withstand these temperatures. Regular everyday glasses, while seeming to be fine, may not be good for candles because they might have weak spots in them that when they get hot, might break, spilling the wax and creating a big safety problem. Therefore recommendations by most of the knowledgeable candle makers is to use high quality glass containers made especially for candles.

Now if you have some old metal tins or cans around the house, they would be acceptable for molds. You just need to spray a mold release on the inside before adding the wax.

For the more advanced candle makers, you can buy things to add to the wax that will change the color, add fragrance, increase the hardness, prevent fading and bubbles, to name a few. None of these are hard to use or find. They just take some experience in using them and seeing their effects.

"Professional" candle making is a progressive art. You start simply, learn the basics and go from there. Once the basics are learned you can experiment with the more advanced techniques and additives, all the while, your expertise is growing as you continue to add to your experience.

Candle Making Recipes Used For Fancy Candles

Even though candle making does have its particulars, when it comes to making candles there are not a whole lot of ingredients required to compete the process. If you are planning on adding colors and/or fragrance to them then you will need appropriate candle making recipes to get the correct proportions of materials added to the mix. With the exception of these two additives, there isn't usually a crying need for any elaborate candle making recipe unless you are looking for exact amounts of wax to make a particular number of candles..

Finding candle making recipes is not a difficult task except for any unusual ingredients that you may be adding, such as embedded objects or previously mentioned fragrances and coloring. Basic recipes can be found at the craft stores, department stores and other various businesses that sell wax or other candle supplies. These candle making recipes range in price

Chapter 3 : Basics of All Candle Making Recipes

but some businesses will have them displayed for free so that you can pick one up and take it home. You can also enhance your options by searching online. They will generally be listed according to the type of wax, the strength of the fragrance, the specific color, and any other additives that you would like to use. Adding to the number of available recipes is the growing variety of additives and enhancements.

Especially important is when you are making candles with strong scents you will need to look for recipes that specify the resulting level of scent strength. Candle recipes can be modified once you have enough experience but because of the proportions that are required when you are just starting out then you should look for recipes specific to what you desire. If you are looking to use other additives aside from color and fragrance you can find those in abundance as well. There are many candle supply companies online that will give you those recipes for free.

Take the time to look through the candle making recipes. There are lots to choose from and you are bound to find the right ones eventually and it may not take but you a few minutes to do so. Candles are fun and pretty easy to make as well, so start experimenting with elaborate recipes. You'll have the fanciest candles and amaze your close ones and your customers.

Making candles is both a rewarding and fun pastime. The art of candle making will bring you many hours of enjoyment and creativity. If you are new to candle making, then there are many things to learn in order to create your masterpiece. Having said that, it is not difficult - you will however need to be organized and have all the necessary ingredients and utensils to make it an enjoyable experience.

Store bought candles can be very expensive, especially the more ornate ones, so why not have a try at making them yourself. You may just surprise yourself at how fancy your candles can be. If you have all of the necessary ingredient and utensils ready to go, then all you require is a good candle making recipe.

There are many candle making recipes to choose from, starting from the basic candle, through to the scented and more elegant candles. Some candles have objects embedded in them and these might be better left once you have acquired a few more skills and experience. If you are new, try to start with a basic candle first. This may be difficult to resist as you may want to make some of the more beautiful candles that you may have seen, however you will definitely be glad you started simpler if your attempts at making a difficult candle fail miserably.

You will be able to find candle making recipes at your local art and craft store, or where you bought the ingredients and utensils from. Often times these store owners will have recipes for free on flyers for you to choose from. The more elaborate candle making

Chapter 3 : Basics of All Candle Making Recipes

recipes you may have to purchase. Search online for candle making recipes also, once again you will probably find a small selection of free simple instructions. This will get you on your way and gathering the experience you need to make those more difficult but beautiful looking art pieces.

Outlaying a small amount for a good candle making recipes book is a great investment. As you gain experience and knowledge and become an expert candle maker, you can recoup your investment dollars by selling your candles. There are many people who are not the slightest bit interested in making their own candles, but do have a love of candles and love to display them around their homes. These people will gladly purchase your candles from you. You will be doing them a service.

Candles are fabulous presents too. If you have a signature or label you can adhere to the candle, all the better as people admire your candles they can see who made them. Put your contact details on the bottom of your candle so that you can reach more customers.

Do try to start off simple and resist the urge to make a very fancy candle when you are new. Starting simple will give you confidence as you progress into a first class candle maker.

Candle Types and Candle Making Tips

Candle Making For Beginners

There are different types of candles you can make. All you need is to follow the simple steps in basic candle making and add a little creativity. The different types of candles are discussed below.

First is the most common type called gel candles. It consists of gelled mineral oils. It appearance is transparent and it feels soft, similar to Jello. This type is placed inside a container.

There are also container candles poured inside a heat-resistant container such as tins or glass and then it is burned inside the container when utilized.

Pillar candle is poured onto a mold ad then extracted, typically having a diameter of about 2 up to 3 inches. Thus, they have 1 or more wicks but they are free standing.

Votive candles are small and cylindrical, about 2.5 inches in height and 1 to 2 inches in diameter. This is placed inside a votive candle holder in order to retain the wax. This is because they liquefy when they are lit.

Taper candles are one of the more common varieties. They appear thin, wider along the base and they tend to narrow upon reaching the top. They are about 6 up to 18 inches in length and they are placed inside a candle holder. They are also called "dinner candles".

Tealight Candles are small cylindrical types filled within a plastic or metal cup. It is about 1 up to 1.5

inches high and 1 up to 2 inches in diameter.

Floating candles are poured onto a mold with various shapes and it is used in a bowl filled with water. They tend to float, adding a special touch once they are lit. This is since wax is noted as buoyant.

Wickless candles are generally poured onto a heat-resistant container, having no wick at all. This is used by placing it on top of a warmer in order to have the scent released without using flames.

Tips in Candle Making

When it comes to the wick, the length and size to be used depends on the size of the candle you plan to make. If you will have a large wick, your candle tends to melt faster. If you will have a very small wick, it will not produce a good light. This means that the size of the wick should be proportional to your candle's size.

When choosing as well as positioning your wick, you need to initially utilize an appropriate size. This should be according to the planned diameter of the candle you will be making. The recommended sizes are 6 to 8 ply or 0.5 inches, 12 to 14 ply or 1 inch, 16 to 18 ply or 2 inches, and 20 to 24 ply or 3 inches.

Make sure you utilize wicks that have larger diameters which do not easily melt. Good examples are paraffin and beeswax.

Candle Making For Beginners

In order to keep a straight wick in your candle's central portion, it is advisable to tie its end onto a stick placed over your container or mold.

The different types of wicks include the Square Braided Wicks best for molded, dipped and container candles; Metal Core Wicks best for container candles; and Flat Braided Wicks best for tapered candles.

When it comes to the color or wax dye of the candles, it is not advisable to utilize the colors used for cosmetics or soap. This is because it clogs the wick. Since adding color or dye to your candles can give it a more personal touch, it is best to make use of concentrated liquid or sold colors. If you will be coloring candles by batches, it is best to use concentrated liquid. A single drop can actually color about 1 lb. of wax.

In coloring melted wax, make sure the candle wax was opaque when it was still solid or maybe even before it was melted. It will then become blear when it has melted and is ready to be dyed or colored. This becomes apparent when the melted wax hardens as it cools. It will turn opaque with its color fading.

Safety Tips on Candle Making

On no occasion should you leave the process of melting wax without assigning someone else to watch over it. This is because was extremely flammable and

Chapter 3 : Basics of All Candle Making Recipes

can cause fires.

If fire should arise, never use water to put it off. It is best to place a fire extinguisher nearby.

Never heat wax to temperatures more than 100 degrees C.

Make sure you are using a reliable thermometer for monitoring the wax's temperature.

Never place the wax directly on the fire while melting it. It is best to utilize a wax melter or double broiler for this process.

When handling the container or kettle with melted wax, always utilize a pot holder so as to avoid untoward accidents.

CHAPTER FOUR

Making Candle Wicks for Candle Making

Have you ever considered making candle wicks as part of your candle making hobby? Yes, candle wicks that you make yourself. With a few basic supplies, you can fashion your own wicks to have on hand at any time. For the serious hobbyist especially, making your own candle wicks can prove to be not only a budget saver, but ultimately a time saver as well. What's more, you can proudly say that your candle creations are completely your own!

The Candle Wick

The candle wick is the most important element of the candle. It's like the engine that makes the entire candle "go." But how exactly does a wick work? It's quite basic actually. When lit, a candle wick will:

Melt wax

Absorb wax

Chapter 4 : Making Candle Wicks for Candle Making

When melted wax is absorbed into the wick, it essentially fuels the flame. Thus a cycle is born in which the flame creates the "fuel," and in turn, the fuel keeps the flame burning.

When making candles, it's important to choose the right-sized wick. A wick that's too small will starve a flame. On the other hand, a wick that's too large will burn too hot and deplete the candle's fuel too quickly.

Generally speaking, a good way to determine the right-sized wick to use for a candle is to consider the size the finished candle will be. A bigger candle will usually take a thicker wick. But there are other factors, such as the type of candle you're making and the type of wax being used, that you'll also take into consideration.

If you learn how to make your own wicks, however, a wick that's the right size is never far. Making a range of wicks of different lengths and thicknesses for storage is a good idea. Wicks wrapped in newspaper will keep nicely and will be on hand whenever you need them.

How To Make Candle Wicks

In one form or another, wicks have been around for as long as there have been candles. In the 19th Century, however, the stabilizing effect of boric acid on candle wicks was discovered, and candle wicks

Candle Making For Beginners

have been made pretty much the same way ever since.

To make your own wicks, you'll need:

- Salt
- Borax
- Water
- Cotton twine/string
- A hand towel/paper towels
- Wax
- Double boiler
- Tongs
- Newspaper

Mix together a batch of boric acid solution from 1 tablespoon of salt, 2 tablespoons of borax, and 1 cup of hot water. Cut lengths of twine, and let them soak in the boric acid solution for several hours.

Remove the twine from the boric acid, and dry it completely with a towel. Next, take three pieces of twine that are the same length and braid them.

Now that you have your twine braided, melt your wax in a double boiler. Using tongs to hold one end of a length of braided twine, dip the twine into the wax. When the twine is thoroughly saturated, remove it from the wax, and dip it in water. Lay the twine flat on a paper towel, and allow it to dry completely.

You now have primed wicks for your candle making that you've made yourself!

To store your completely dried wicks for future use, simply roll them up in newspaper and set them aside in a cool, dry place until needed.

Tips: You can repeat the process of dipping the twine in wax to achieve a slightly thicker, stiffer wick. Cotton kite string works well as the twine used to create your wicks.

Candle Making and Interior Design

Candles create the perfect atmosphere in the home and gives off the needed ambience in the living area and the bedroom. The use of candles for interior design helps encased a romantic feel to any room; with flickering lights and the aromatic scents to give any room a sense of life and bursting passions. It gives dramatic impact, to make a room look cozy and inviting. The visual appeal of candles set the right mood, luxurious feel, holistic wellness, and romance in the air.

Candles can aesthetically complement the decor of any room. They light up a large space with just flickers of subdued light. Unique candles encased in either wicker, wrought iron, metal and glass can give any room a sense of style and elegance. The aroma that they give off, depicts the personality of the homeowner - vanilla and lime essences for a country feel ambience; and musky and flowery scents to connote a sense of romance and style.

Candle Making For Beginners

Candles as interior decor can be used even if the homeowner is on a limited budget. There are many inexpensive aromatic candles that can be bought for a few dollars. These are found in several online stores and local retail outlets in the area. There are many decorative candle designs that you can choose from: pillar, totem types, column, decorative or scented candles.

Candle Making as Alternative Option

Candles have been a part of man since ancient times. Some have used it for emergency lighting and as decorative tools for the family home. Making candles is fairly easy to do. It will need a few basic ingredients, tools and equipment. There are many types of candles; but basic candle making remains the same. The basic guidelines are as follows:

Candle making safety

These would include safety tips like: never leave burning candles unattended, flammable materials should not be placed near the flames, use of candle holders, keeping matches and candles out of reach of children and many others.

Candle Making Techniques

Perfecting the candles may need a lot of experiments

Chapter 4 : Making Candle Wicks for Candle Making

and testing. Beginners are advised to keep track on their work outputs to avoid making the same mistakes again. There is need to keep a log on the following:

The source of the materials that are used. This includes the manufacturer's name on the labels of every material - wax, fragrances, wick, wick holders, dyes, pigments, containers and other ingredients.

The quantity of the product used and tracking time for cooling and addition of materials into the mixture.

Imperfections that may be observed - cracks, air bubbles, discoloration and others.

Effect of scents on the mix as to subtlety or potency. There should be clear observations on the intensity of the scents during burning time since it may lose its scent once burned.

Careful observation of the burning time of the candle. How long it last and the quality of flicker for each time. There is need to observe the flame - whether big, small, or if it drowns in wax or smokes.

Testing should be done in smaller batches to save on materials and supplies.

Soy Scented Candles

Soy Scented Candles are becoming more and more popular as people realize the benefits that they bring.

They are environmentally friendly, coming from a renewable source (the soybean plant) rather than its rival, the paraffin candle which comes as a by-product from refining petroleum. They burn a much cleaner flame, emitting less soot, last longer and are easier to clean than paraffin. Combined with a lead free wick and you're on the way to creating the perfect candle.

So with all of the benefits of soy wax, it has become a great ingredient to use in candle making. With a little bit of thought and experimentation, you can create your own unique soy scented candles with wonderful aromas to fill your home or make them as beautiful presents.

The basic step-by-step making of soy candles is easy. First of all melt about a pound of soy wax (flakes are easier to work with) in a double boiler. When that is completely melted, remove from the heat and add about an ounce of your chosen fragrance oil (we'll look further into this aspect in a moment) and stir in well. Then add your dye, again stirring well. Pour the melted wax immediately into your prepared molds, with the wick in the center (wicks with the metal disc's attached are often the easiest choice) and center the wick by using a pencil. Once the wax is set and hardened, remove from the mould (if necessary), trim the wick and enjoy! Remember during the whole process to never leave the wax unattended while it is over the heat.

Chapter 4 : Making Candle Wicks for Candle Making

The fun part is creating your unique scent and style. Search the web for great deals on fragrance oils or if you've got a good hobby store near you, they should hold a big enough selection. Why not think about a combination of complementary scents such as Apple Pie and Cinnamon? Enjoy experimenting and create exactly what you are looking for although it may take a few goes to get this perfected. If you prefer a stronger scent, simply add more fragrance. Then think about the color that you want the candle to be. If your scent is chocolate, you may want to add a brown dye color to create an overall aesthetically pleasing candle.

With your scent and color chosen, have a look around your home for items that would make good molds. A pretty jam jar or a decorative ceramic flower pot, are just a couple of examples of everyday items that would make great candles. There are a great range of molds also available on the internet and in hobby stores if you'd rather. If you are creating a fruity scented candle, think about adding some pieces of actual fruit to the candle, or if you're doing a coffee scent, add some coffee beans, although always remember to double dip any additions to your candle in wax: So before you start, dip that piece of fruit in the wax and leave to dry before later adding to the candle. Cherries, raspberries, leaves, coffee beans are examples of accessories that will give your candle that extra wow factor.

Finally, to make it even more unique, why not think

about a layered candle? My favorite idea at the moment is a season's candle. So, if started in October, I may want a Pumpkin Pie scent to burn initially, moving into my second layer for November when I think a nice Short Bread scent would remind me of all the Pie baking, and moving into December where a nice Cinnamon scent would be Christmas-y. That's just one idea. If it's springtime, think about combinations of Floral or Fresh Linen scents. A Chocolate scented candle in an egg mold would be perfect for Easter. Be creative and have fun with the process.

Layered candles are easy to prepare. Divide your wax into three and begin by melting a third of the wax and adding the scent and color that you would want at the bottom of the candle (or top depending on what type of mould you are using). Allow this to set until there is a film on the wax. Then prepare your next one third of wax, choosing your scent and color carefully, pour this into your mold and then repeat this step with the final amount of wax.

With a bit of creativity, you will truly be able to create soy scented candles that are sweet (or whatever your favorite scent type is) and definitely unique.

Reasons Why Scented Candles Have Become So Popular

Candles have been around for many centuries and

Chapter 4 : Making Candle Wicks for Candle Making

before electricity and gas, they were the main source of lightning for people around the world. Today, candles have made a big comeback, in particular scented ones and they have become extremely popular, especially with women. Scented candles are widely available and many shops have sprung up in the high streets and shopping malls as well as online. The price of these special candles is somewhat more than your standard ones, but the lovely scents and beautiful colours more than justify the expense.

Scented candles have become very popular as gift ideas and many people have switched to candles as birthday and Christmas presents as opposed to the usual perfume and soap gift sets. You can get scented candles in many different shapes, sizes and colours and some are even a mixture of colours and fragrances which is why they make such ideal gifts.

When it comes to making you home feel more relaxing and inviting, you can't go wrong with scented candles and they are perfect for almost every room in the house. They are great for creating a romantic night in front of the TV with the lights turned down or off, or for use in the bathroom to help you relax and unwind while you have a well deserved soak. Many scented candles come in small glass jar type containers and you can even buy frosted-glass patterned candle holders which when you turn down the lights, create lovely silhouettes on your walls using the candle's flame. So treat yourself or a friend to a scented candle

Candle Making For Beginners

as we all deserve time to step back from our hectic lifestyles and relax once in a while.

I didn't have much desire to make my own candles for the longest time. I was perfectly content with buying my favorite candles over and over because they did the job. I enjoyed them, and I figured that there was no reason to even attempt making my own candles when the experts seemed to have it all covered. On top of that I figured it would make an absolute mess of my place (anyone that has tried cleaning wax from their carpets knows what I'm talking about).

The thing is.. when I finally decided to take that leap and had finished making my first candle I realized that I not only didn't find it that hard, but that I had just found a new hobby that I REALLY enjoyed! Part of the reason I was finally convinced to try and make my own candle was because of the great work that companies such as Candle Science do by putting out their candle making kits for beginners. Getting started is really as simple as buying one item on Amazon and waiting for it to arrive at your door. I was sold!

If you are still on the fence about whether to give candlemaking a shot or not than reading through the following list might help you come to a decision.

You Can Let Your Creativity Run Wild!

Making your own candles can be as simple or complex as you would like it to be. There are no rules as to what you can and can't do with homemade candles. Sure, some of your ideas might not turn out as well as you'd hoped, but it teaches you to learn and improve in your next ones!

The various techniques that are out there when it comes to making different types of candles are endless and still, to this day, are growing and evolving. For example: just have a look at this video on Youtube by Kimberly of Natures Art Handmade. So great! And finding new techniques like this are part of what makes it all worthwhile.

Know EXACTLY What Is Going Into Your Candle

With the ever growing concerns of having eco-friendly and safe ingredients in products that are around us, making your own candles becomes an even better option. Many of the candle companies have adapted to the changing of times and are now using these ingredients more often but you still can never know for sure unless you make it yourself.

There are still many ongoing debates as to if certain wax types are more harmful than others but regardless, you can decide this for yourself and go with what you think is best.

Choosing Your Own Fragrances or Creating Your Own Scent Combinations

This point may go along with the previous one but I think it deserves it's own place on this list.

When it comes to the scent of a candle, no two people will have the exact same tastes. Fragrance intensity is also one of the factors that will cause the biggest differences in opinions for all candle lovers. Some people love candles that are so strong that they can throw fragrance around an entire room even before they are even lit, while other people prefer when you can just get faint hints of scent here and there.

Candle companies can't cater to everyone's needs and therefore making your own niche candles is a great chance to experiment. Have a scent that you want to go after? Think about the key ingredients that go into making it and test out combinations of fragrance oils that will create it. The sky is the limit!

They Are Fun and Easy To Make!

Again, if you don't know where to start I suggest grabbing a beginners candle making kit. You will have everything that you need and after that, it is as simple as restocking on the ingredients you used up and making more! You will feel like an expert in no time.

Tips on How to Make Your Own Scented Candles

It always feels great when you create something

Chapter 4 : Making Candle Wicks for Candle Making

yourself and use it as well, rather than just buying it from the market. Candles have always signified elegance and beauty, and the best part about them is that they can be very easily created by you at your own home in any shape, size, color, and design you choose. You can even add your favorite fragrance by using scented aromatic oils during preparation.

There are many varieties of candle making wax available in the market, each with different features, you will first need to evaluate the features of each of these waxes and choose the one which completely suits your needs. Paraffin wax is generally used for most homemade candles.

By following these simple steps, your very own scented candle will be ready in a couple of hours:

Fill a pan slightly with water and let it heat on a low flame. Take a container, put the wax in it, and keep it in the middle of this pan filled with water. Allow the water to boil.

Note: Do not boil the water on high until it starts bubbling as this may cause the water bubbles to splatter in the wax.

As soon as the water starts to heat, the wax will slowly start melting. When this happens, dip a thermometer into the melted wax to measure if the temperature reaches 175 degrees. As soon as it reaches 175 degrees, pour the melted wax in a dry bowl or a coffee

Candle Making For Beginners

mug.

Note: While dipping the thermometer in the container, make sure that it doesn't touch the sides or bottom of the container.

Now you can add the color chips into the melted wax. It is always recommended that you add a few color chips at first, because if the wax color becomes too dark, it will be very difficult to bring it back to a lighter shade, but if the wax color is too light then there is always the option for you to add some more color chips later.

Add your favorite fragrance to the colored wax, in the form of aromatic scented oils which are readily available. Always use only half a teaspoon of scented oil while candle making, because using any more can create problems in your candle burning efficiently. Make sure that you continuously keep mixing the wax as you add the scented oil so that it mixes evenly. Transfer the mixture into your wax mould slowly and keep the remaining wax in the hot water pan so that it remains hot.

Just as the mixture cools, the wax will begin to reduce. Keep adding more of liquid wax to it till you are sure that the desired candle size has been achieved. Simultaneously, keep poking the candle gently with a skewer several times at ten to twenty minute intervals, as doing this will add air into the candle that will help it keep its shape when removing it from the mold.

Chapter 4 : Making Candle Wicks for Candle Making

After about 4 to 5 hours you can try removing the candle from the mold and if it still sticks to the mold then place it in your refrigerator

Note: Do not place the mixture in to the freezer as it will lead in cracks to your candle

In order to put in a wick, poke the skewer again into the center of the cup as the wax begins to glide. Every time you insert the skewer, turn it several times so that you prevent it from sticking to the wax.

Normally it is very easy to insert a wick, but in case you are unable to, then dip the wick's bottom a little bit into the melted hot wax and then try fixing it to the center of the candle, this will ensure that it is straight at the end that has to be shaped. You can trim it depending on the length of the entire wick.

Soy Candle Making

Soy candles are candles made from soy wax, which is a processed form of soybean oil. They are usually container candles, because this wax typically has a lower melting point temperature than traditional waxes, but can also be made into pillar candles if certain additives are mixed into the soy wax.

In candle making circles there are mixed views and feelings about the relative merits of soy and paraffin wax.

The supporters of soy wax will argue that soy candles are cheap compared with their only real natural wax rival - beeswax. Soy wax is a new alternative to paraffin which is not only cost effective but is also made from a renewable source.

Soy wax is all-natural (apart from the necessary additives, of course, which may or may not be natural!) This new wax is a favorite of environmentally-conscious people because it is not made from petroleum, like paraffin candles. Burning of soy candles does not increase the carbon dioxide level in the atmosphere.

There are claims that soy candles can last up to 50% longer than paraffin candles. This has never been properly tested and as there are so many variables it remains debatable. Most candle makers will know that the speed at which a candle burns down can depend very much on the size and type of wick used - larger wicks generally give a fiercer and more quickly burning candle.

Wax spills are easier to clean. It's very difficult to remove paraffin wax from furniture or textiles whereas soy wax spills can easily be cleaned up with hot soapy water. This ease of cleaning up is also a definite advantage from the candle maker's point of view.

It is argued by some advocates of soy wax that soy candles produce less soot and that what soot is produced is a less harmful white soot. This is still debatable and there seems to be no definitive answer as to the truth of black and white soot!

Scented soy candles distribute more fragrance - The incorporation of soybean oil lowers the melting point of the candle, which translates into cooler burning candles and faster scent dispersion. The lower melting point of this type of wax results in a larger size of the liquid wax pool around the candle wick. It is from this liquid wax pool that the essential oils evaporate into the atmosphere. This argument seems to be logical, so there may be some truth in it.

There is however, no arguing with the fact that soy container candles are very easy to make and if you are happy with a container candle, rather than, for example, a pillar candle, then soy wax is one of the easiest waxes to work with.

The Health Benefits Of Soy Candle Making

The benefits of soy candle making are plentiful with full emphasis of it being the source of good health. Candles are becoming one of the most favorite choices for gifts and favors for people around the world. They have evolved into an assortment of mesmerizing designs, styles, shapes and various other eye-catching patterns that has swooped the world off their feet.

Candle Making For Beginners

However, out of all the different types of candles, soy candles have become immensely popular in the past few years. It was in 1991 that Michael Richard brought in soy wax, and today this has become the best alternative for other kind of waxes.

The aroma of the warm soy candle is very appealing as the candle radiates light and can create a tranquil ambiance. These candles have become the most preferable choice because they burn longer and are quite affordable.

Surprisingly, not many people know that these candles come with a lot of health benefits. For those who enjoy making soy candles, some of the benefits are:

No soot: when a regular candle is burned, a powerful gas known as carcinogens is released into the air. This is a very harmful toxin. A lot of studies have proved that carcinogens are a major cause for cancer, and other health related problems. These candles are natural and do not emit carcinogens.

No chemicals at all: The Environmental Protection Agency has identified the presence of two cancer-causing agents - toluene and benzene to be present in paraffin wax. This when inhaled, causes high risk of cancer, and several other health disorders! However, benefits of soy candles making allows you to have no chemicals at all.

Safe to touch: today soy is found in many products

Chapter 4 : Making Candle Wicks for Candle Making

like a lot of soaps, lotions and even hair care products. Hence, soy candles are safe for your skin and they are safe to handle. This cannot be assured in case of paraffin wax and any other wax material.

Environment friendly: with global warming on the rise, candles like these contribute a lot to the environment. These candles emit no smoke at all, which is great for the environment, and also for people inside the house. These candles help to maintain good quality air inside the house and for people who have breathing problems these are an excellent choice.

Allergy: a lot of people are allergic to smoke and various other chemicals that are released from candles. Soy candles are perfectly healthy and do not produce any irritating gasses that can trigger allergies.

The benefits of soy candle making are many and the market has produced numerous varieties and designs in them for you to explore. These tempting designs and the fantastic aroma has made the demand skyrocket in the last few years. With more awareness, people are resorting to such kind of candles for their homes

Quality Candle Making Scents Make Better Fragrant Candles

Scented candles are in huge demand and are admired by the young and old and male and female populations around the world. But few know that these scented candles do come in variations and the differences mostly seen in the quality of the candle making scent itself. Candle making scents come in various qualities and choosing among them dictate the quality your candles.

Scented candle fragrances can be purchased for $14 per pound to $3 per pound. Wonder why do they come in such a difference? Well, the answer to this is that the higher the concentration of a fragrance, the more expensive is its ingredients and its formula. However, if you go in for inexpensive fragrance the ingredients too are of a cheaper quality along with a very simple formula.

It has been universally proven that quality candle making scents make better candles, and if you are into making candles as your hobby, then you probably should know that choosing the good quality candle making scents will definitely result in a better quality candle and a greater looking artifact.

Then again if you are selling candles for a business or plan to, it is best to use quality scents because they throw a better fragrance and although they are a little dearer to purchase you do not have to use as much because of their concentration.

The benefits of choosing better quality candle making scents

Better wax quality: when you choose a good quality expensive fragrance for your candle then you definitely cannot compromise on the quality of the wax you purchase. This is why a better quality wax along with a better quality fragrance result in better burning candles. Moreover, expensive fragrances have expensive ingredients in it, which results in a better and long-lasting fragrance.

Less dangerous: lower quality candle making scents might have cheaper ingredients and can include fillers and other impure elements that can result in a dangerous flame. Many studies have proven that most of the cheap scented candles available in the market have dangerous ingredients in them that result in severe health problems. Even though candle making scents might be a bit expensive, you can definitely ensure that they are extremely safe for health conditions.

Versatility: good quality candle making scents come in a variety of complex scents that might not be available in cheap quality fragrances. Good quality candle making scents come with fine quality concentrations like perfumes. You might also enjoy pleasant smells like vanilla, sandalwood, lavender, and gardenia. Those are only a few fragrances as there is a very long list to choose from.

Buying good quality candle making scents is definitely the wisest decision to make extremely good candles, and if you are thinking about transforming your hobby into a home-based business then you definitely need to resort to these types of quality control to ensure that you build a loyal customer base and get repeat trade. Customers definitely look out for cheaper products, but when they realize the advantages of good quality candle they will come back for more.

How to Choose Your Candle Making Wax

Paraffin Wax

Paraffin wax is the most common form of candle wax, as approximately 94% of candles purchased at a retail outlet are made from this material. Candle makers usually use this type of wax as it is relatively inexpensive when compared to the other types of candle making wax. Paraffin wax is often sold in 10 lb. or 11 lb. blocks which are not always of the same shape, size, color, or surface texture.

Beeswax

The second most popular type of candle making wax is beeswax. Beeswax candles are extremely easy to make and quite popular due to their natural aroma which resembles honey. In addition, beeswax candles last longer than paraffin wax candles, and can be purchased in blocks, sheets, beads or chunks. Many people choose to make beeswax candles as the beeswax sheets do not need to be melted, and can be rolled or molded into candles by hand, without the use of heat or electricity.

Soy Wax

Soy wax is one of the newer types of candle wax, and is 100% natural. It is made from a pure natural soybean base and contains no herbicides, pesticides, additives or preservatives. Candles made from soy wax burn cleaner than other types, burn more evenly, last longer, and have little carbon build up. Because of this they are generally thought to be less dangerous to pregnant mothers and people with allergies. In order to keep the candle 100% natural, soy wax candles are usually made with pure essential oil fragrances, rather than with synthetic scents. These candles are often used as aromatherapy candles.

Palm Wax

Soon after the development of soy wax, palm wax was created. Palm wax is one of the more expensive types of candle making wax, however some people are willing to pay more as this material burns with no soot and is easy to work with. When used alone for candle making, palm wax offers clear, stable colors, burns for a very long time, and is considered a high quality wax. Palm wax is often used in conjunction with other types of wax, as it is expensive but helps give other candles a more polished finish.

Gel Wax

Gel candles are made out of gel wax, which is essentially gelled mineral oils and plastic polymer. Due to its high flash point, it is not recommended for beginner use. These types of candles usually feel quite rubbery and are transparent or semitransparent, and often contain bubbles. Non-flammable objects can be placed inside for decorations, making these the most fun types of candles to create.

Bayberry wax

Bayberry wax is an uncommon wax made from berry shrubs. This expensive wax is made from the Northern Bayberry and Southern Bayberry and offers a beautiful natural aroma. Its soft green natural color is often used in conjunction with beeswax, which brings down the cost but doesn't compromise on quality.

Regardless of what type of wax you choose to use, make sure you choose the right one for your project. Doing your research now will save you time and money later.

CHAPTER FIVE

Candle Making Business

So what do you need to know to start your own candle making business? This is a question that I get a lot and it has both a simple and a complex answer. The truth is that starting your own business is tough, however, when it comes to crafts like soap or candle making or even knitting or quilt making, it can be easier than other options that require less skill and are not as practical or personal.

There are a few simple things that need to be considered when you are thinking about starting your own candle making business, the first of which is to honestly answer the following question, "How much do I enjoy making candles?" You need to make sure that you enjoy making candles enough to run your own business, if you begin making a lot of candles and find it to be boring and no longer enjoyable, then it is time to reconsider making it a full time job. Now this is not to say that there is not going to be times when you are not enjoying it, but if these feelings start as you begin to up the production of candles then you may want to stop.

Another thing to consider when starting your own candle making business is that you need to start slow in order to make sure that the candles that you make are even worth selling. They need to be of decent quality and come at a fair price. How do you know if your candles are worth the time and energy that comes with running your own candle making business? Start by hosting a small party, invite all of your friends and family, as many people as you possibly can. Make sure that there is good food at the party, some nice music, and a lot of comfortable places to sit and talk.

When your guests arrive at the party give each of them a card with questions about the candles, questions like:

"What do you think about the quality of the candles?"

"What do you think about the fragrances of the candles?"

"How much would you willingly pay for the candles?"

Think of some more questions that have to do with the candles you have made. Make sure to tell your guests that they should not put their names on the card and to be honest with their opinions, also, ask for any specific suggestions. Have a basket prepared and let everyone place there cards in the basket when they are done. Make sure you give everyone some candles before they leave.

When everyone is gone take the time to read

everything that all of your guests had to say on the cards. Take the time to improve your candles and evaluate the suggestions of your friends and family members. When your candles are new and improved host another party and this time explain that you will be selling the candles. Make it like a Tupperware party, where people can come and enjoy the party and also buy some candles. If the party is a success then begin to start selling the candles on websites on the internet, also start selling them at arts and crafts fairs.

These are the first steps to starting your own candle making business. Once the candles are doing well at fairs and online, you can start your own website that sells them, create a brand and really advertise your candles. Once the website is doing well then you can always get an actual store front or get a cart at the mall, the choice is yours. Remember that when you are starting your own candle making business that you should have fun but remember to take it slow and do not quit your day job until you have a decent amount of income coming in.

Make Unique Candles At Home

Many people are looking for unique candle making ideas and for good reason, when you have been making candles for as long as I have you start to develop a desire to create candles that are new and interesting. This is not to say that making the same type of candles that you started out with is ever going to get boring, it is just that sometimes you need a change in order to improve your candle making skills and spread your wings in terms of creativity. So what are some unique candle making ideas that you can try?

Well one of my favorites is making candles with crayons, this is very easy to do and you pretty much make these candles the same way that you make normal candles with only a few slight differences. For example, you use crayons as the wax. All that you have to do is to remove all paper wrapping from the crayons, put them in to some boiling bags, place the boiling bags in to a pot of boiling water and that is it! In about ten minutes the crayons will melt in to colorful wax, feel free to mix and match colors or put like colors together to make your own creation.

As far as unique candle making ideas go have you tried to make your own candle molds? The mold that you use for your candles will go a long way. All that you have to do is to get some clay and create a mold for the candle, just be sure of two things. First make sure that the mold is made in such a way that you can actually get the candle out when it dries, if the mold is shaped in such a way that the bottom is bigger than the top then you may have trouble. Also, in order to solve the problem that was just mentioned you can always make a mold that you are going to break after one use, so when the candle dries you simply break the mold away from it.

Chapter 5 : Candle Making Business

Another one of the unique candle making ideas that you can try has to deal with the way you resent and make your candle, for example you can make a floral scented candle and use a flower pot as the mold. Or if you want you can use gel candle wax, use a fish bowl as the mold and place sea shells at the bottom of the bowl. One of my favorite unique candle making ideas has to deal with sea shells, simply take a sea shell and pour candle wax in to it and then stick the wick in it, this creates nice little sea shell candles that are perfect for decorating your home or parties.

Candle making is an old age craft which has been in existence for so many years. Candles were first made to satisfy two purposes of providing heat and as a source of light for seeing and appreciating our environment. The above stated reasons for inventing the candle remain the same even thousands of years after.

The methods of making candles have changed considerably over the years from the earliest method of making candles from twigs tied around a stick to rags tied around a stick and dipped in a flammable liquid to the present wax candles.

Over the years there have been different products that have been used for making candles, such as one of the most recent, gel wax. Gel candles have proven to be very popular as they can be made to look so beautiful given some practice and with the various embeds they can be made to be very personal as well.

One word of caution though, is that all wax that is being melted on an element needs to be done with care. Candle wax has a flash point and if the temperature is not controlled with a thermometer a serious fire can be caused.

When starting out making candles it is important that if the melted wax methods are going to be used that the hobbyist takes the time to learn about:

- what equipment is needed
- how to melt wax, safety precautions
- how to prepare the molds
- other parts of candle making before they start their new hobby

Two other parts of the candle making technique which a beginner candle maker needs to learn about before starting is the adding of color and candle scent. These also need to be done with care and it is best to remove the wax from the heat before adding them and to stir them in with a wire whisk as this mixed them through the best.

Some popular candle types that beginners can make are:

- pillar candles (round or square)

- ball candles
- votive candles
- floating candles
- ice candles
- beeswax candles

Generally speaking, votive candles are the easiest to start with as they are small and not a lot of wax has to be used to get good results. It is possible to buy a set of molds in a silicone tray and this does a great job or otherwise an investment in six single molds would work well.

When a beginner starts out they do not need to invest a lot of money in molds and can start making their first pillar candles in waxed milk cartons and these work really well. It is just a matter of peeling the wax carton away when the candle is set.

Beginners need to do a little experimenting to start with and the great thing is that all wax can be remelted so nothing is wasted. I hope these candle making basics have helped you get a picture about starting candle making and that you enjoy your new hobby.

Candle Making Crafts for Any Holiday or Special Occasion

Candle Making For Beginners

Who doesn't love candles? Candle making crafts are a fun way to celebrate special occasions by making them more memorable with your customized candles. You can use old canning jars, broken pieces of crayons with a bit of essential oil for fragrance, gel candles embedded with seashells or other found objects and hand dipped candles for an elegant table setting. For the bride and groom you can make unity candles with personalized messages such as a scripture, a special poem or the couple's initials.

Stacked pillar candles:

This type of candle making crafts uses leftover wax. Melt the wax and add fragrance and color as desired. Lightly spray silicone on a cookie sheet. When the wax is about 175 to 185 degrees F pour it on the cookie sheet and allow it to cool. When the wax cools to a consistency of cookie dough use a cookie cutter to cut out shapes. Poke a hole in the center and leave to cool completely. Thread a pre-tabbed wick through the holes and push down all the way on the wick tab. Arrange the shapes in any design you wish. You can melt the top of each shape with a heat gun for better adhesion.

Cupcake candles:

Cupcake candles are great for birthdays. Melt wax, add fragrance and dye and place cupcake cups inside of a muffin pan. Pour wax into the cups almost to the top when it is about 140 to 145 degrees F. When the wax is starting to cool you can insert pre-tabbed wicks. When completely cool peel the cupcake cups away and place the candles on a cookie sheet. To prepare the whipped frosting wax, melt wax, add fragrance and coloring as desired. Whisk the wax as it cools until the color lightens and it looks like whipped cream. At 85 to 90 degree F scoop the wax up to the top of the cupcakes and use a fork to get the desired look. For syrup melt wax, add dye and allow cooling until thickened. You can add wax hearts or other decorations to get unique candle making crafts.

Tilted layer candles:

Great for Christmas as they look like candy canes. Melt the wax, wick your mold and fill a box with sand digging a hole large enough to fit the mold and place it at a slight angle with sand packed around it. Pour the initial layer of wax at 180 to 190 degrees F. Allow the initial layer to cool and pour the second layer about 10 degrees hotter. Repeat steps until wax is near the top of the mold, upright the mold until it is standing straight in the sand and pour the last layer. Allow to cool completely and remove the candle from the mold.

Why You Should Absolutely Learn Candle Making at Home

You know you have always wanted to learn how to do candle making from home but for one reason or another you have put it off. Maybe you think it will be too expensive or that its too complicated, you could never learn. Possibly you think you will have to buy a whole bunch of specialized equipment. Then I have great news for you! Read my list of reasons you absolutely should try candle making at home.

Less Expensive

Making your own candles at home will cost you a fraction of what it costs you to buy candles from retailers. When I have shopped for candles I have been shocked to look at the price of them. $49.00 for one simple candle? You have to be kidding, right? Wrong! Candles purchased ready made are very expensive and a real luxury item if you live on a fixed budget as I do. Instead, by purchasing your candle making supplies in bulk, for instance wicks and waxes, you can produce equally gorgeous candles for just pennies a candle.

Choice

When you make your own candles at home, you have the choice of what style, color, scent and shape you wish to have. Store bought candles give you very little choice. You may find the right candle color but the scent puts you off. Or you find a price you can afford but the color is wrong. Candle making at home allows you to choose all of these options yourself. These options are only limited by your own imagination.

Kid friendly

Candle making at home provides you with a great opportunity to spend quality time with your children. Clean up is a breeze if you plan ahead and when properly supervised, children will love making their own candles using their own unlimited imagination. This is especially true when making gel candles where the ornaments are inserted right into the candle wax.

Therapeutic

Teaching yourself a hobby or a craft is wonderfully therapeutic for you. While your hands are involved in your craft, your mind relaxes and tensions flow out of your body. You forget about your daily problems and focus on the creativity of creating your own beautiful candles. If you are anything like me, you will find that any problem that you might be struggling with will likely resolve itself during the time you are making your candles. Working in the background, your mind is free to mull over the problem without interference from the red flags and objections your ego will raise and by the time you are finished your first project, you will likely find that your brain has come up with a solution to the problem.

Customized Gift Giving

There is nothing better in the whole world then to receive a gift from someone who obviously cares about you enough to take the time and thought to create your gift. Hang on! That is incorrect. There is one thing better and that is being the one who gives that customized gift. When gifting a candle to someone you love, you can choose exactly the right color, shape and scent for this special person. For instance if you know their favorite color is pink and they love the smell of vanilla, you will be 3 steps ahead in creating an ideal gift for them.

Home Based Business

Homemade candles are becoming one of the fastest growing home based businesses around. That is particularly true right now with everyone scaling back on their household expenses. Decor items like candles are usually the first to get cut from the shopping list. When you are able to make beautiful candles for just pennies of what the retailers charge, your customer list will explode. Craft fairs, flea markets and even your own online storefront are not beyond your reach when you become a master candle maker.

Equipment Easily Found in Your Own Kitchen

Unlike other hobbies and crafts, the equipment required for candle making at home is short and

Chapter 5 : Candle Making Business

contains items that you will probably find in your own kitchen, basement or garage. If you make gel candles, you may require an additional piece of equipment called a multi-cooker but otherwise, everything you need to make your own candles you probably already own.

Beautify Your Own Home/Power Outages

Making your own home cozy and pleasantly scented is easy as pie when you make your own candles. You can choose exactly the right color, shape and scent to use for each room to compliment your existing decor. And what about the candle-lit baths made extra special because the candles were handmade by you and the color and scent are made exactly for you.

Furthermore, during power outages, instead of having paid way too much for a package of plain white candles to light your home, you will have a very plentiful stock of your own candles in different colors and scents to light your home while waiting for the power to come back on. It can be very romantic during these outages instead of being an inconvenience.

Easy to Learn How

Candle making is one of the easiest crafts to learn how to do. I have taught myself many crafts including crochet, knitting, scrap-booking and pottery. By far, candle making was the easiest of them all to teach myself. With the right book, the right supplies and equipment and just a little bit of creativity, you can be making candles the same day you begin.

Lends Itself to Pursuing Other Crafts

Once you know how to make stunning candles, you will be amazed at what other crafts you can use your new found knowledge with. You will be empowered to discover new crafts that you've always wanted to try but possibly didn't think you could learn how to do. There are a myriad of crafts that you can use candle making for such as making Easter eggs, Halloween candles, your own birthday candles and the list goes on. Learning how to make candles at home can literally change your life!

CHAPTER SIX

Candle Making Wax

Wax is the most important ingredient in making candles. Without it candles will not be complete. There are many candle making waxes that you can choose from, such as paraffin, gel, beeswax, soy, and palm. They can be bought easily online and in local craft stores.

The rising types and styles of candle wax have caused a huge increase of interest in this amazing hobby.

One of the most common waxes is paraffin. Paraffin wax is made from refined petroleum and often has a white, shiny finish in its solid state. Because of its popularity this wax has become affordable and widely available.

Another type of candle wax is natural wax. Natural waxes are products of nature. It is usually produced from palm, vegetable, soy and bayberry.

For an eco-friendly candle making experience, soy wax is a good choice. It is a renewable resource and needs a lesser amount of production energy. Soy wax is produced by the process of hydrating soybean oil. Most people prefer soy wax in making candles because they produce cleaner soot and their spills are easier to clean. Compared to paraffin wax candles they also last and burn longer. Soybean is not a hard crop to find, it is commonly grown in some states in the Midwest part of the US.

Other sources of candle making wax are animal sources. An example of this is beeswax, a natural wax produced from the beehive of honeybees. Candles made of beeswax are a bit costly but they are also health friendly. Candles made out of this wax produce less pollution. When burned, it also creates a pleasant honey-like smell. It also lasts longer, hypoallergenic and burns cleaner. It also gives a calming and relaxing effect to its users.

Gel wax is another type of candle wax. It comes from mineral oil that has been formed into wax using a plastic polymer. Gel wax produces candles with clear and transparent look and rubbery texture. Candles made out of gel wax are also called jelly candles because of their jelly-like trait. Gel candles also burns out slowly compared to regular wax candles. These candles are fun to design because of its transparency. You can suspend items and accents in the wax to produce beautifully decorated candles. Gel wax is available in three densities, low, medium and high. Low density gel wax holds lesser fragrance load. It can only hold 0.3 percent fragrance. Medium density gel wax can hold a fragrance load of 3.5 percent while high density gel wax can hold the heaviest load among the three. The higher the density of the gel wax used

Chapter 6 : Candle Making Wax

the more fragrance it can hold.

Having the knowledge on different kinds of candle making wax can give you many options to choose from when you decide to make your own candles. To spice up your creations, you can add accents, styles, fragrances and colors to your candles. In candle making you can explore without limitations. You can also discover more kinds of wax and explore what designs suits them best.

Wax is the most essential ingredient in creating candles, without it candles will be incomplete. The most common type of wax used in candle making is the paraffin wax. It is refined petroleum with a white, waxy and solid feature. It is widely used in candles because it is readily available and inexpensive.

Another popular choice for making candles is natural wax. It is produced from natural resources such as palm, vegetables, bayberry and soy.

Soy wax is an environmental friendly wax. If you are a person with high regard for the environment then this is the perfect wax for you. It is a renewable resource that comes from natural sources. This wax is produced by hydrating soybeans which is a common crop in the Midwest United States.

Another renewable wax is the palm wax. Although this is natural and renewable it still causes environmental destruction in other countries such as

Malaysia and Indonesia. Large areas of rain forests are destroyed to produce more palm plantations. This eventually results to loss of habitat to rain forest animals and extinction of plant and animal species.

Waxes for making candles is not limited to refined petroleum and plant sources. There are also waxes that are animal based such as beeswax. Although this type of candle wax is expensive, many still prefer using it because of its pleasant smell, strength and burning characteristics.

Another type of wax is gel wax. This type of wax has a rubbery texture and gel-like features. It is available in three densities. The type of gel wax density that you will choose will determine the type of fragrance you want to achieve for your candle. The higher the density of the wax the more capable it is to hold a heavier fragrance load. A gel wax with a low density is able to hold 0.3 percent fragrance load while medium density gel wax can hold a 3.5 percent fragrance load.

Knowing the different kinds of waxes available is an advantage for candle makers. With that knowledge you will have many options and you will be able to make different kinds of candles for different people, situation and occasion.

In candle making you should also experiment with different kinds of wax. As you discover the uniqueness of each kind of wax you can also add styles, designs and fragrances to further improve your creations. You can also make different candles for business and gift giving. You will not only experience the joy of creating candles but you can also produce products that are income generating.

Why You Should Choose All-Natural Candles

Many of us enjoy burning scented candles in the home. It helps to provide an air of comfort and can mask some of the more difficult odors that may exist in the home. Although it is certainly possible for you to use many commercial scented candles for this purpose, that doesn't mean that they are the best choice that can be made. Unfortunately, many candles are manufactured with chemicals that can actually be harmful to our health. They may smell good but the effect of the candle can be toxic. What are some choices that you can make which will help you to use candles without that concern?

One of the main reasons why scented candles are bad for you is because of the paraffin that is used in creating them. Paraffin releases chemicals that can cause cancer when it is burned. Although most people don't realize it, it is a waste product that is produced in the petroleum industry. Burning a paraffin candle in the home is similar to running a diesel engine in your house and breathing the fumes. The effects of burning this type of candle can be severe and can lead to cancer and respiratory problems, such as asthma.

All-natural candles, on the other hand, are made with soy wax. You can burn these candles in the home and enjoy what they have to offer without worrying about the negative effects that are produced with paraffin candles. This is not only going to be seen in your health, it is also seen in the cleanliness with which they burn. Many paraffin candles produce black soot that can be seen in the direct area where they are burning but it will also be throughout the home. Soy candles, on the other hand, are clean burning.

Another part of the candle that you should consider is the wick. Many of the commercial candle companies use wicks that have lead cores. Most of us are familiar with the fact that lead is bad for you and burning lead in the home can release chemicals that will end up in your lungs. In choosing all-natural candles, you will be using a wick that is lead-free and will not produce the same problems when it is burning.

The scent of the candles should also be considered when making your choice. There certainly are many commercial candles that smell wonderfully when they are burning but that doesn't mean that they are burning cleanly. Those scents are produced chemically and artificially. That is why many people are unable to burn candles because it causes an allergic response. Natural candles, however, use natural ingredients to create the scents that you will enjoy.

Along with those problems that may occur with many

Chapter 6 : Candle Making Wax

commercial candles, you should also consider the other toxic chemicals that may be in the candle. There is a long laundry list of dangerous chemicals that can cause reactions in the body that are severe. Quite obviously, making the right choice in the candle that you burn is going to benefit you and your family.

CHAPTER SEVEN

Reasons To Make Your Own Homemade Candles

Homemade candles are beautiful items to decorate and to add fragrance in rooms of your house. Moreover, there are less chances of chemical and toxic outburst, since you make your own candles, deciding which materials to use and which to not. These are pretty easy to make and quite beautiful to look at when they are lit. And most importantly who doesn't want to show off the deep seated skills they have. Interestingly, there are plethora of homemade candle ideas that you can possibly use to make your very own candles. Homemade candles are good as a gift item too. You can give your near and dear ones candle gifts.

There are a variety of homemade candles. You can pick the one that suits you best.

Luxury Candles:

If you are looking for luxury candles in any supermarket, it may cost you a lot, as price varies from $20 to as much as $400. You can find these from renowned supermarkets but ideally you can make your own luxury candles. But the fact remains

Chapter 7 : Reasons To Make Your Own Homemade Candles

that the process of making luxury candles is almost the same as making of any candles. And the equipment is also the same. What you need as an extra piece of equipment is the unique material that will make it luxurious. Most of the people add fragrance and colour to make luxurious candles. Candle scents can be found in any candle supplier's shop and you can choose best colour that suits your taste best.

Candles for Less:

There are a variety of choices for candles for less budget. You can make your own homemade candles just to lighten the house or to decorate your house. Most of the waxes that are found in the market cost less, and it makes candle making more affordable.

Taper candles:

There could be found no candles as elegant and sophisticated as taper candles. These are easy to make and you can, in fact, make taper candles of 6 to 24 inches if you wish. You can use your homemade taper candles just to lighten up your house or these items are good for decorating drawing room, kitchen and your living room.

Beeswax Candles:

Beeswax candles are renowned for their long lasting burning time and the golden glow they produce while burning. As beeswax candles take more time to burn itself, it is advised to use thick wicks. However, the procedure of making homemade beeswax candles is the same as making of any homemade candles.

Olive Oil Candle:

Olive oil candles are very easy to make. All you need is a jar, olive oil (you can even use expired olive oil to save money) and a wick. Set the wick at the middle of the jar. Tighten the wick with the bottom of the jar with a thick piece of rolled paper or heir clip and tie the top part of the clip with another clip or something that you feel comfortable with. Now pour the olive oil in the jar. Now it is ready to be burnt.

Floating Candles:

Floating candles are great items to decorate your living room. It is different and unique.

Candle Scents:

Candle scents are widely used items to add extra appeal to homemade candles. There could be found a wide variety of scents in candle suppliers' shop. They offer a wide range of scents. Seasonal, fruits, foods and drinks, flowers, holidays and events scents are mostly common among candle makers. You can also choose from Amaretto, Amber Vanilla and Coffee etc. Additionally, there are scents that are similar to that of major perfume manufacturer like CK, Polo, and Obsession etc. The price of these scents varies significantly and 16oz of Obsession scent can cost you around $17, for example.

Now it is time to make Candle Gifts. Have you ever thought of gifting your homemade candles to your near and dear ones? It is really an awesome experience to showcase your craft and get live feedback. Truly speaking, homemade candles are beautiful items as a gift. These are very pretty to look at, if these are prepared with care and craft. Prepare your own homemade candles and wrap those with beautiful wrapping paper or with your DIY wrapping cloth and now your candle is ready to send as a gift.

Benefits of Making Candles Instead of Buying

Making candles can be an extremely rewarding and fulfilling activity. Candles are great to have on hand for a variety of occasions, making them versatile and practical home décor items—not to mention useful tools in the event of an electrical blackout. Candle-making can be fun and interesting and once you learn the procedure, and the benefits of doing so are many. Here are the 5 main benefits of making your own candles instead of buying them.

Save Money

Making candles at home is a great way to save money. Not only will you not need to buy your own candles, you can also save money on gifts for friends and family. Buying supplies in bulk will help you to save money on raw materials you need for this project.

Make Money

Not only can you save money, but you can also make money by making your own candles. Setting up a home-based candle business can help you to supplement your income while doing what you love. If a business sounds too big and complicated, you can start off by hosting a candle stall at fairs and community events. In fact, you can start an online store that operates out of your own home without needing any extra space or room. Scented candles, personalized candles and uniquely shaped candles are just some of the examples that can draw the crowds in. Candles are needed all through the year, so there would be a constant demand for handcrafted candles.

Reasons Why Every Home Should Have Candles

Every home is special to each person in their own way. The feeling home gives you is always comforting, safe, and warm. They say home is where the heart is and we truly believe that at M. Boutique. There are many things that could be done when turning a house

Chapter 7 : Reasons To Make Your Own Homemade Candles

into a home. Aroma, beauty, and tranquility are all things that make up each person's unique homey feel, and candles can achieve each of these things.

Aroma

Everyone has a certain smell or aroma that reminds them of home. Whether it is the citrus of neroli lotus, or the sweet scent of lavender, we all know a smell that reminds us of home. Burning scented candles throughout the home add to the comforting feeling of home. M. Boutique has a variety of scented candles to choose from to help make your house smell like home.

Beauty

Another factor that turns a house into a home, are the aesthetics of the home. Décor is important in making your home feel inviting and comfortable. Some flickering candles throughout your home is known to be visually pleasing and ads to the beauty of the home itself. Use candles as a decoration, and not just a smell diffuser. Pair them with other interior decorations to make for a truly beautiful home.

Tranquility

Home is always a place you can unwind and relax. After a tough day a work, or a long time of being out of the house, it is always a great feeling to step foot in your home and instantly feel at ease. Burning candles gives off a tranquil vibe of relaxation and gives your home that comforting feeling that every home should have.

These are just a few of the major reasons every home should have candles. Make your house something more by adding a comforting aroma, visual beauty, and calming tranquility and turning into home.

Candle Making as Therapy

Hobbies are a great way to de-stress and calm the mind. Craft projects like candle making can be therapeutic and can help you to wash away your tension and stress easily and naturally. Spending time with wax, wick, colors and perfumes or essential oils while creating something that you love and enjoy is a surefire stress-reliever. In fact, if you make scented aromatherapy candles, you can light them up each time you're feeling stressed and tense. Inhaling the soothing fragrances will help to calm your mind and lift your spirits.

Fun Craft for Kids

Candle making can be a fun way to spend summer holidays and rainy days with older kids. Since candle making involves dealing with hot wax, it isn't a good idea to try it out with young children except under careful supervision. However, tweens and teens can be trusted to exercise caution while having fun making candles. Engaging in creative hobbies like candle making will help children to develop their own imagination and have fun while doing so.

Candle Making Can Be Eco-Friendly

Although paraffin wax is traditionally used for candle making, it does increase pollution and leaves an unhealthy impact on the environment. Instead, you can go green with your candles and make them from natural soy wax. Soy candles have a naturally nice fragrance, are relatively inexpensive to make and have a natural sheen and smoothness to their texture. Beeswax is also an eco-friendly option for candle making; however, it is more expensive than both paraffin and soy wax.

Candle making can be fun, therapeutic, eco-friendly and economical. Whether you make candles to give as gifts, to sell at the school fair or simply to create something lovely, the advantages of making your own candles are reason enough to engage in this creative hobby.

CHAPTER EIGHT

Ways to Use Candles

Here are 5 simple ideas to help decorate your home using candles.

- Create A Spa
- Dining
- Bedrooms
- Livingrooms
- Mantels

Create A Spa

Soaking in a hot tub of water will help to erase the days stress. Create your own simple, spa looking, bathroom by using these simple ideas.

Place a small, soy pillar candle on a candle plate that compliments the color of your bathroom on your counter add a single bud vase with a fresh cut flower. This will give you a fresh clean look.

If you have enough room on your bathtub, decorate the front ledges with tall and short pillar candle

Chapter 8 : Ways to Use Candles

holders that have white pillar candles on them.

If there is not enough room, simply place votive holders with votives or tea lights in them around your tub.

Dining

A dinner lit by candle light is simply romantic. Whether you are going to have a candle light dinner or not, decorating your dining table with taper candles creates an elegant aurora.

Use unscented taper candles so that you are not distracting from the fragrance of your dinner.

Center your taper candles for your focal point and place decorative items around the base of your taper candle holder.

Create a dramatic effect by using a candelabra.

Have fun with kids and help teach them romance by eating peanut butter sandwiches by candle light.

Bedrooms

Bedrooms are a place for relaxing. Adding candles can help create a more relaxing mood.

Accent your dresser with a pillar candle

Place decorative candle holders on your nightstand

Candle Making For Beginners

away from your bed.

Place a lavender scented soy candle in your votive holder. It is said that lavender helps in relaxing.

Light your candle 30 minutes prior to bed time to fill you room with the lavender scent.

Make sure you extinguish the candle prior to going to sleep.

By placing a pillar candle on your dresser with You can simply place a pillar candle on your dresser to add a simple touch to your other accessories, or you can place a decorative votive holder with a candle on your nightstand. Whether you are going to light your candles or not, Lavender scented candles make a great scent for the bedroom. Lavender is thought to help aide in relaxation. If you are not keen on the idea of a lavender color candle in your bedroom see if you can purchase candles without color.

Living rooms

Most living rooms are the center of gathering for family and friends. Adding natural wax candles allow you to add color, accent, and romance all at the same time. You can add contrast to your living room by grouping several pillar candles together using different sizes in diameter and heights. Place the group on a large plate making sure that you have at least one inch between your candles if you are going to light them. Find colors that complement the color of your walls or even a throw pillow on your couch.

Mantels

Decorating fireplace mantels is fun with candles. By grouping both taper and pillar candles of different heights and diameters together you can add a dramatic visual effect. You can easily change the colors to match the season.

Decorating with candles is a simple, cost effective, accessory to any home decor. You are only limited by your imagination. When decorating with candles, remember to always place pillar candles on a heat resistant surface in order to protect your counters and furniture. Always place votive and tea light candles in proper containers. You can be more eco-friendly by incorporating natural wax candles throughout your home.

Using Candles As Garden Lights

As summer begins, many of us are wondering how we can make our yard and garden look warm and inviting at our next gathering. The answer is candles! Candles are a great way to add depth and warmth to your patio, yard, and garden. There are many ways in which homeowners can use candles to complement their exterior décor. To help you create an inviting atmosphere, I have put together some great ideas on how you can use candles as garden lights.

We've all seen the plain clay planting pots at the home improvement stores and many craft stores. But what many homeowners don't think of when they see them is that they make great candle holders for your yard. They are relatively inexpensive and come in a variety of sizes that will allow you to be creative with your lighting. You can simply fill the pot with sand, rocks, pebbles, or shells to create a base for your candle to sit on. Depending on your décor and the type of gathering you are having, you can even use colored sand to create a festive look. You may also choose to simply fill the pots with candle wax and make your own candles. If you have any candle making experience this can be a relatively easy DIY project.

The next decorating idea is to place different sized candles in hanging mason jars. Mason jars are the latest hot trend and they can now be found in a variety of colors and sizes. When you use mason jars as candle holders, you should place a small amount of sand in the bottom of the jar. This will help keep your candles stable and secure should a breeze pop up. If you have a lot trees or even a gazebo, you can easily hang these jars and provide your yard with a sense of wonderment and warmth. This is a great idea for barbecues, family dinners, and parties.

How many of you have seen the large displays of different shaped glass jars and bowls in your local craft shop? These bowls and jars are ideal for using as

candle holders. Because they can be fou
large sizes, you have the option of filli
with rocks, shells, and water. If you
water and any of the other decorative elements l
listed, you can then use the bowls and jars to hold
floating candles. These can then be placed on tables,
bars and other seating areas to create a warm and
inviting look.

Use Candles in a Wedding Ceremony

A person's wedding is the most awaited occasion in their lives and thus they wish for it to be perfect. It takes several months of planning for the preparation of a perfect wedding ceremony, which involves things like selecting the wedding gown, sending invitations, using the right flowers, hiring caterers, choosing a perfect chapel for the wedding, making a proper seating and table arrangements, etc. There is so much to take care of that sometimes we tend to ignore the very little things that can make your wedding a unique and elegant.

Something like using candles innovatively for your wedding ceremony would be a great idea to start with. Lighting up candles signifies peace and additionally relaxes the atmosphere of the wedding. Mostly, candles add a decorative element that can you're your wedding stand out from other weddings. There are so many ways in which you can use candles in your wedding.

Let's have a look at few such ideas:

Having a candle light theme at your wedding ceremony is a great idea. The only part to take care of in a candlelight wedding ceremony would be that you make sure to have all the necessary information regarding the fire code for the location where the event is held and to see that all the rules of safety are followed. Candles also add a lot of glow to the entire atmosphere. Also candlelight is very romantic and everyone enjoys the warm glow of candles.

You could also place these candles across the path that leads to the wedding chapel. But everyone passing through the path especially the bride needs to be very cautious about the fire on the candles. Make sure to place the candles far apart enough so that people can easily walk along the pathway.

Candles can also be used as centerpieces for each table in the wedding reception hall. There are several ways in which you can place these candles innovatively with specific decorative themes. You can use them as part of a larger centerpiece or you can create a candle arrangement with a larger candle in the middle and smaller candles on the outside.

You can always make the venue of your wedding reception unique by placing large bowls or basins of water on each table with floating candles in it. Floating candles can be found in many varieties to suit many different styles of weddings. It is advisable to

Chapter 8 : Ways to Use Candles

use at least ten candles for a large bowl and somewhere around five candles for a small bowl.

Of course last but not the least, placing a uniquely designed candle on your four layered wedding cake would give an absolutely unbelievable look and feel to the occasion. You can either choose to make it yourself giving it your own personal touch or have them custom made for you. You can even get wedding favor candles in various themes. Sometimes, favor candles are small enough to place on your wedding cake.

Hence candles should definitely be a very important ingredient in your wedding planning, as this would be a very beautiful and elegant way to spend the most important day of your life.

Use Candles to Spice Up a Night at Home

Spicing up a night at home together can easily be done with the help of a few candles. A room lit only by candles is a perfect atmosphere for romance. Not only is it romantic, but everyone looks amazing in the flickering hot fire of candlelight. Of course candles are always used primarily to set the perfect lighting in a room but they can actually be used for much more.

The scent of a candle can create a certain mood as well. Burning all fruity smelling candles may put you in a fun, flirty and playful mood together while floral, tropical smells may remind you both of your romantic honeymoon you spent together on the beach. Scent is an extremely powerful memory trigger so choosing a perfect scent can really go a long way in spicing up a night together. There are also specific candles available that contain Pheromones that are highly recommended to set the mood.

Massage oil candles can really enhance a steamy evening together. Candles are available that have a wonderful, sensual, massage oil created after they have been burning. These soft warm wax substances smell phenomenal and feel amazing on your skin. Looking for a real treat? There are also edible massage oil candles for you to experiment with. These candles allow you to have four senses intrigued; sight, smell, touch and taste.

Candles that are created specifically for the bedroom are made from natural products like soybean oil, fragrant oils, almond oil, vitamin E and Shea butter. The idea behind these is that after having hot wax dripped on your body, it can be rubbed into your skin. Not only does it feel amazing but it is good for your skin too. Traditional candle wax can be irritating to you your skin, hard to scrub away and impossible to get off of fabric and out of your hair. Special bedroom candles may cost a bit more but they are well worth it.

For some people, being romantic comes easy, for

Chapter 8 : Ways to Use Candles

others, it doesn't. Candles set a mood for you. They are a a representation of affection, just as much as roses, jewelry, chocolates, etc. Walking into a candlelit room automatically transports you somewhere else, away from your busy day and stressful worries.

Couples that not only use candles for lighting purposes but that experiment with special types of candles that produce sensual oil give themselves the ability to take their special evening together to a much spicier level.

Decorate Your Home for Valentine's Day Using Candles

Saint Valentine's Day is the most romantic day of the year. The national holiday has become the official day for lovers. Individuals, who know the secret to making love last, know that you have to make efforts to show your object of affection love everyday of the year. Nevertheless, making your partner feel extra special on this day is a fun opportunity to unabashedly show your love and appreciation.

There are many great ways to celebrate Valentine's Day. You can go the traditional and expected route; dinner and a movie. But everyone else will be doing this. Subsequently, restaurants are packed and waiting hours on end to be seated is hardly romantic. Instead of battling the crowds, you might want to consider staying at home and creating a beautiful and intimate experience of your own. This article will provide you with some great ideas to help you decorate your home and set the mood for Valentine's Day. It is very easy to add a bit of romance to your home by using inexpensive things like candle and flowers.

Candles are an easy and nearly instant way to set a romantic mood. Place candles strategically around your home. Candles add a soft, romantic glow and besides, everyone looks good in dim lighting. For safety reasons, be sure to use candle holders and keep candles away from flammable material. Being forced to call the fire department, or having to scamper out of a burning house, can really ruin the mood.

During this time of the year, you may want to consider using pink and red candles. If you are going to be eating in, set the table with scattered rose petals and tall, ivory candles. Floating candles in a nice crystal bowl can also be quite beautiful.

Fragrance is also is another way to evoke romantic feelings. Take into consideration the tastes of both you and your partner. If you love a particular fragrance, purchase it for this special night. If you or your partner are not necessarily "candle people," you may want to make a few dry runs. Go and buy some candles and burn them so you that you get an idea about what scents that you like. The scents that get the highest marks get the go ahead for Valentine's Day.

Chapter 8 : Ways to Use Candles

When decorating your home with candles for Valentine's Day, don't restrict yourself to only using single candles. Instead, try tying a few candles together with a piece of beautiful ribbon. This will greatly multiply the glow from the flames, resulting in a beautiful and dramatic effect.

Now that we have discussed candles, let's talk food. Chocolate, strawberries, chilled champagne (or your favorite cocktail) and a few aphrodisiacs, helps to complete the mood. Before the big night, choose a special poem or write your own, have your partner do the same. On Valentine's Day read them to each other by candle light.

Valentine's Day is a time to go all out for your partner. Do your best to make it special. Staying at home and creating a romantic setting allows you to fully enjoy each other, while not having to fight the crowds. Using candles is the perfect way to add to the ambiance.

Things To Think About When Using Candle Lighting

When you have finally decided to use candles as a light source for your lighting fixtures, it means that you need to be more attentive to some aspects of your décor more than others. It also means that you will have a different method of using those light fixtures than usual. For starters, when using a light source that does not rely on electricity, you do not need to worry about the electrical cords and wires running from the electrical outlet to the light. But there are also other considerations.

One thing you will need to be aware of is the melting wax. Candles naturally burn the candle wax down as they burn through the wick. So where does the melted wax go? It goes down of course. If you are going to have a candle lantern (for example), then you will need to make sure that you plan for what you will do with the excess wax buildup. And if you are going to hand your candle lights above your head, you need to worry about wax dripping onto you and your guests. Additionally, with an open flame as your light source, you will need to make sure that it stays away from flammable items such as curtains.

Aside from the physical and safety measures, you will also want to pay attention to the décor of the room. Since candle light flickers, it can cause light and shadows to dance about in the room. This can cause a room that will look one way in conventional lighting to look completely different in candle light.

Make sure you are clear about the type of lighting that is best for your room. Candle lighting can help improve the look and feel of your room, as long as you do your homework before purchasing them.

Using Candles As Fireplace

Decorations

Whether you are using your fireplace on a regular basis or if the weather has become too warm, your fireplace is still the focal point of your room. To help you ensure that it looks great all year long, I have some helpful ideas on how candles can liven up the space even when there is no fire going. Placing tall candleholders and candles are a great way to elongate your fireplace. They catch the eye and force it to look up, which can create a dramatic effect in your living room.

Holidays are a great time to decorate your fireplace with candles. You don't have to go over the top, but you can celebrate the holidays in a subtle manner with some carefully chosen candle designs. When decorating for the holidays, you don't want your candles to be overwhelming. To keep this from happening in your home, you should choose smaller sized candles that you can place on your fireplace along with some small decorations. This is enough to create the festive look you were going for, without overdoing it.

Any time throughout the year, a simple row of candles in glass jars can create a warm and pleasant atmosphere. Not only will they add warmth to your room, they can also be used as an accessory to your décor. Glass candle holders can be found in a wide variety of colors, sizes, and designs which will easily match your décor, and add to it. If your room is somewhat drab, you can use these multi-colored glass holders as a way to add some much needed color to your room.

If you've always wanted a fireplace but have never had the chance to have one, you can simply create a faux fireplace in your home. To do this, you simply need to build the exterior mantle of the fireplace against one of your walls, creating a deep open space in the middle. Once you have done that, you can then place different candle holders of varying heights in that open space. This is a great way to experience the look and feel of a fireplace without actually having one.

During the holiday season, you may be a bit worried about using real candles around your decorations. To help put your mind at rest, you can always use flameless candles. These candles are designed to create the same atmosphere as real candles, but without the flickering flame that can be dangerous. These are also great options to use in your home if you have pets or small children.

How to Make Candles in a Variety of Designs

Now that you know how to make candles, you have to make it stand out. To make your candle unique, you must learn ways to design it. For those who want to learn how to make candles with different designs, there are several things you can use: stamps, stencils and wax.

STAMPS

Using a stamp is actually an easy and effective way to decorate your candles. Just about any kind of stamp can be used, with any design. All you have to do is apply paint onto the surface of the stamp and stamp away! It is important that you don't put on too much paint on the stamp, or else the design might get smudged. If you make a mistake with the stamp, you can easily wipe the paint off the candle, as long as the paint hasn't dried yet.

It would also be a good idea to first practice stamping on some regular paper before you actually stamp on the candle, so you get an idea of how hard you have to press the stamp. Also, remember that a candle is usually round; thus, when applying the stamp, roll the stamp onto the candle surface, following the contour of the candle.

STENCILS

Many people favor the use of stencils in designing candles because stencils tend to produce more professional-looking designs. There are stencils available from arts and crafts stores that you can use, but make sure that you pick flexible ones that you can wrap around the surface of your candle. You can also make your own designs and cut it out.

Once the stencil is placed snugly around the candle, you can use acrylic paint, spray paint or stencil paint to fill in the design. Carefully paint the sections that have been cut out. Let the paint dry out a little before gently removing the stencil outline from the candle. If you make a mistake, you can remove the excess paint by scraping the candle wax little by little. When you have finished filling in the stencil, you can now add some fine details into the design, such as other colors or elements.

WAX

Since you already know how to make candles, using wax to design your candles will be quite easy for you. Use candy molds or cookie cutters to create the designs. Just as with candle making, melt the wax until it becomes liquid, after which, you pour it into the mold. Let the wax cool and harden. When it is ready, take the shapes out of the mold. Paint some melted wax onto the back of the shapes you have created, and press them onto the candles. Use a hair dryer to help the shapes curve around the surface of the candle. Let it dry for about 24 hours. Finally, you can add some embellishments to make the design really different.

CHAPTER NINE

Candle Making Equipment

If your a candle making wiz the following information may come to you as old news. When you are ready to start making candles, various types of equipment will be needed. Whether a novice candle maker who enjoys filling the home with wonderful fragrances or a professional candle maker, creating amazing masterpieces, you will find candle making equipment specific to your needs.

Melting Pots

A small melting pot is ideal for the hobbyist. This size pot will hold up to two pounds of melted wax and can be used on direct heat or with a steamer pot for the double-boiler method. This method is the best option for reducing potential hazards, by controlling the wax temperature and not allowing it to reach dangerously high temperatures.

The standard melting pot is like the smaller melting pot except it holds up to four pounds of melted wax. This would be ideal for craft parties, making holiday candles, or for average-sized projects. Again, the double-boiler method is recommended.

The steamer pot is used with either the small or standard melting pot as the double-boiler piece of equipment. This method is often preferred since the wax does not have to be monitored as closely. The double-boiler method eliminates the wax flash point, where temperatures can reach 400° F and catch on fire. With this method, wax never exceeds 210° F as long as the water level is kept at the recommended level.

If preferred, you can choose a wax melting kit that usually includes a small melting pot, steamer pot, thermometer, and wooden sticks. If you are a serious candle maker, equipment is available to make the process easier.

For example, the 50-pound electric melter melts up to 50 pounds of wax in two hours! This melter is economical and features a temperature control dial and replaceable flow control valve. Most types of wax can be used with this melter although plain wax works best for easy cleanup. To add color or fragrance, use a separate container. This greatly reduces inside cleanup. When the melter needs cleaning, melt plain wax, running it thorough the valve until the wax flow is clear.

The 150-pound wax melter melts up to 150 pounds of wax all at once. Not only does this take time off production, but it also increases profit. This model is designed to use heated water to melt wax safely and

Chapter 9 : Candle Making Equipment

fast. Features include a water level indicator, see-through lid, dual water drainage plugs, water temperature display, and replaceable flow control valve and heating element that includes a temperature control dial. This too should only be used for plain wax, using a separate container for color and fragrance.

To increase the quantity of candles being made, you can step up to a 100-pound wax melter, designed to melt up to 100 pounds at one time. Features include two temperature control dials, and a replaceable flow control valve. For wax type, cleaning, color, and fragrance, follow the same pattern as the 50-pound model.

Dipping Vat

Dipping vats come in various sizes for different needs. The single tank, dipping vat is not heated and perfect for a five-inch taper dipping ring. This vat holds up to 25 pounds of wax and can dip 10 candles at once. For the wicks, holes will have to be drilled into the mold or the candles themselves.

The dipping ring is designed for 10 candles and can be used with the single tank or the 7-tank dipping vat. To create tall taper candles up to 16 inches, simply adjust the ring.

The large water-dipping vat is the monster of dipping vats. This vat is heated and designed to melt any type of wax safety. The features on this vat include a water drainage plug, extra heavy power cord with grounded three-prong plug, removable tank for easy cleanup, and a replaceable heating element with temperature control dial.

Thermometer

To become skilled at candle making, producing quality candles, you need a thermometer. When it comes to candle making, guessing wax temperature will not work. These thermometers are designed specifically for wax and are very sensitive. You will discover various models but when buying, look for a thermometer that has numbers easy to read, and preferably, one that comes with a sheath to provide protection while being stored. Another feature that comes in handy is an attached ball, which acts somewhat like a small handle, allowing you to turn the thermometer to read the temperature without touching the hot thermometer itself. Most thermometers will have a metal clip, which can be attached to the melting pot so there is no worry about it slipping down into the wax. Generally, wax thermometers will range from 75 to 400° F. If you have trouble finding a thermometer in the wax supply section, look in the candy making section since they use the same type of thermometer.

Stirrers

Chapter 9 : Candle Making Equipment

As the wax begins to melt, you will have some melted wax and some chunks of wax not melted. Wooden stirrers are excellent for stirring the wax not melted around, ensuring the wax melts evenly and at the same temperature.

As you can see there's a array of candle making equipment out there and we just listed a few.

Some of the things you can use, you'll probably be able to find at home, which would be very convenient! Other things you'll have to hunt for either online or offline. You may want to borrow some candle molds from others or even create some of your own to be truly unique! If you're resourceful, you may even be able to substitute some items to save money and time. With the popularity of this hobby, many craft stores carry starter kits that have the essentials needed for basic candle making.

As your candle making skills improve and you start to get more ambitious, then you'll be able to upgrade your candle making equipment. After all, your candles will be so popular with family and friends that you'll have to make more of them and may even consider selling them. Nevertheless, get your notebook out because you'll need to start writing down these essentials:

Basics

Candle Making For Beginners

- melting pot
- stir sticks
- candle mold
- candle mold sealer
- mold cleaner
- digital scale
- thermometer
- wax/gel remover bottle
- mold release spray
- candle gloss coat
- wick pin
- wax scraper
- wick clip
- mini white scoops
- wick trimmers
- wax!!! (soy, paraffin, beeswax, etc.)

Extra

- Additives
- Dye
- Fragrance
- glue dots
- Base leveler - straightening out crooked candles
- Warning labels for proper burning

1. A heat source - something along the lines of your kitchen stove.

2. Container or pot - This is to melt your wax in. In

order to melt wax you will need something that will act as a double boiler, so that you can melt the wax gradually and consistently.

3. A thermometer - To keep an eye on the temperature to avoid it becoming to hot and blowing up all over the kitchen!

4. Candle molds - These can be any size or shape, the only thing holding you back is your imagination!

5. Dipping Can - These are used to dip the wick into the wax, which you need to do for certain types of candle making.

6. Kitchen scale - so wax can be weighed if you want your candles to look the same every time, or if you need a specific amount for a specific mold.

7. Baking pan - Bring out the baking pan to get the wax off of your molds.

8. Cutting instruments (scissors, craft knife etc) - Something sharp is imperative in regards to cutting wicks or wax.

9. Hammer and screwdriver - For larger blocks of wax, use like a hammer and chisel to break it apart easier.

10. Mold sealers - To plug up the hole in which your wick has gone to stop any wax escaping in the drying procedure.

11. Releasing agent or mold releases - Works like vegetable oil when used in cooking - prevents wax sticking to the sides of the mold.

12. Wax glue - To add extra frills onto the sides of the candles. Ribbons, sequins, stickers - the choices are endless!

13. Wick tabs - A small round metal piece which you thread your wick through to help it attach to the candle and also helps it to stand upright with greater ease.

14. Fire extinguisher. - Just to be on the safe side! You never know what can happen when working with wax.

Candle Making Supplies Tips and Tricks

If you are quite thinking on how to start your own candle business, the following sources of candle making supplies will relatively help. In fact, with just a few bucks, you can start your own enterprise and create lovely homemade candles.

Minimal cost is all you need when it comes to starting your own home based business. The start-up can be easier once you can directly associate your passion for candles and earn money out of it.

Here are a great number of candle making supplies tricks and tips.

Chapter 9 : Candle Making Equipment

- Get started with a candle making kit. Yes, you heard it right. A candle making kit provides one with the essentials of homemade candle making. A typical kit normally includes wax, spoon, and a thermometer. It may also include measuring tools, cutters and wicks.

These candle making supplies are normally available in the net. Other sources likewise provide users with various types of fragrances and dyes for candles. Soy candles, in general, are easier to make because of these kits. All you have to do is inquire, learn the basics and comply with the requirements set by each kit.

- It is also best to equip oneself with a double boiler as such is needed in wax melting. A sauce pan can also be used as a replacement. You can also make use of two pans as an alternative.

- Investing in a large pot is also necessary. This tool is important not only in melting your soy wax but it also keeps everything organized and easy to clean. For instance, choosing a non-toxic, stainless steel pot is usually recommended as part of your candle making supplies list. This item is also highly-preferred as compared to aluminum pots and containers.

- When it comes to dyes and fragrances, you

can choose from a variety of options such as liquid colors and scents. Be reminded though that while each item has its own benefits, the results are still considered the same.

- As for other types of candle making supplies, you have to remember that options vary and are not really limited. Sets of fragrances and colors do come in many scents and shades. Supplies stores and craft shops are also some of its many sources.

It is also best to choose complimentary colors and go for fragrances that go well with each candle dye or shade. For example, white or off-white candles go well with vanilla scents. You can also make use of chamomile or lavender fragrances to complement purple-colored candles.

CHAPTER TEN

Making Your Own Wicks

Wicks that are sold by foot are cut at home according to the candle height. Keep in mind that you have to cut a piece that's a bit longer because you'll be tying one side of the wick in order to keep it straight while you're pouring wax and while the candle is cooling. In case you bought a raw wick, you can wax it yourself. You just dip it a few times in hot wax in order to prevent bubble-release from the wick after the wax is poured. There are also auto wick pins, used for making molded candles in molds that are not made with wick holes.

Everything You Need to Know

Making candle wicks is really easy and vital to successful candle making at home. While most people think of a candle's color, shape or fragrance as its most important feature, most candle manufacturers would probably instead say that it's the wick that makes the candle. A candle wick is string, cord, or wooden object that holds the flame of a candle. The purpose of the a wick is to deliver fuel or wax to the flame. A candle wick works like a fuel pump, drawing the fuel (wax) to the flame. Once the liquefied fuel, generally melted candle wax, extends to the flame it then gasifies and burns. The candle wick influences how the candle burns and different sizes of wicks allow for different amounts of fuel to be drawn into the flame. Too much fuel, the flame will flare and soot or too little fuel, the flame will sputter out.

Significant features of the wick include diameter, rigor, fire-resistance, and tethering.

Wicks consist of bundles of fibers that are twisted, braided or knitted together. These fibers absorb the liquefied wax and transport it to the flame by capillary action. Large diameter wicks will result in a larger flame, a larger pool of melted wax, and the candle burning faster. Some wicks may contain a stiff core. This core was usually made of lead, but obviously due to concerns about lead poisoning, lead wick cores have been banned for several years in the U.S. by CPSC. Now, zinc is commonly used a safer replacement for a stiff core although other core stiffeners, such as paper or synthetic fiber can also be used.

Most candle wicks are coated with wax to provide the initial fuel source when the candle is first lit. While the wick is used up in the candle burning process, the true fuel for the flame is the melted wax. Therefore, all wicks are treated with various flame-resistant solutions in a process known as mordanting. Without this processing the wick would be burned by the flames and the flow of liquefied wax to the flame would discontinue.

Wicks are occasionally plaited flat, so that as they burn they also coil back into the flame, thus making them self-consuming. For tea lights, the wick is bound to a piece of metal to block it from drifting to the top of the molten wax and burning before the wax does. Candles fashioned to float in water necessitate not just a tether for the wick, but also a seal on the bottom of the candle to prevent the wick from wicking water and quenching the flame. In many birthday candles, the wick is a nub. This restricts how long the candle can burn.

There are more than one hundred specific wicks in the marketplace today. The candle's size, shape, the wax used, the fragrance materials used and color all impact which wick type to is to be used. Selecting the correct wick is crucial to making a candle that burns cleanly and properly. Reputable candle manufacturers take great care in selecting a wick of the proper size, shape and material to meet the burn requirements of a particular candle.

Types of Wicks

In general, wicks can be divided into four major types:

Flat Wicks:

These flat-plaited or knitted wicks, commonly formed from three parcels of fiber, are very uniform in their burning and coil in the flame for a self-trimming result. These are the most generally used wicks, and can be typically found in taper and pillar candles.

Square Wicks:

These braided or knitted wicks also curl in the flame, but are more rounded and a bit burlier than flat wicks. They are preferred for beeswax applications and can help inhibit clogging of the wick, which can occur with certain types of pigments or fragrances. Square wicks are most often used in taper and pillar applications.

Cored Wicks:

Plaited or knitted wicks employ a core material to keep the wick upright or straight when burning. The wicks feature a circular cross section, and the employment of different core materials allows for a range of stiffness effects. The most often used core materials for wicks are cotton, paper, zinc or tin. Cored wicks can be found in jar candles, pillars, votives and devotional lights.

Special and Oil Lamp Wicks:

These wicks are specially fashioned to match the

burn characteristics of specialized candle applications, such as oil lamps and insect-repelling candles.

Approximately 80 percent of the wicks manufactured in the United States are made of all-cotton or cotton-paper combination's. The balances are chiefly metal and paper cored wicks.

The metal-core wicks occasionally found in candles are generally zinc or tin core wicks. They are most often used in container candles and votives to keep the wick upright when the surrounding wax liquefies. Technological analysis has repeatedly proven both zinc and tin core wicks to be safe.

So there you have it. Everything you needed to know about making candle wicks. Now you can feel completely confident in choosing and making the perfect wick for your candle.

Which Wicks to Use When Making Candles

When you begin to assemble the supplies that you will need to begin making candles, you will be very surprised at just how many different wicks there are. It can get a little complicated to choose which wicks to use when making your candles.

It is extremely important that you choose the right wick. If you make the wrong choice, your candle might not burn well or it might not even stay lit.

Candle Making For Beginners

Picking the wrong wick would be a total waste of your time and money.

Let's go over the different types of wicks. Wicks are either pre-tabbed or they are sold on spools.

Pre-tabbed wicks are used in container and votive candles. They are very stiff and they come in varying lengths with a metal base attached. A long metal piece, referred to as the wick collar or neck, connects the tab to the wick. These long metal pieces also come in various lengths.

The sole purpose of the wick tab is to extinguish the flame once the wick has burned down to the metal neck of the tab. This prevents the flame from continuing to burn and overheating and possibly breaking the container.

Spooled wicks are often used in pillar and taper candles and are purchased without tabs or you can attach the tabs by hand.

The materials that wicks are available in also vary. They can be made from cotton, hemp, paper or with metal cores. Each of these different types is used in certain situations and they offer different benefits.

You also must take into consideration the type of wax you will be using. Some wicks will not work with some types of wax. When you purchase wicks for your candles, you can ask your wax supplier which

Chapter 10 : Making Your Own Wicks

type of wick to use. They can make suggestions for proper wick choices. Some wick will burn too hot or not hot enough for the type of wax you are using so it is important to know which wick will work best before you start.

You can also do research regarding the different wicks and which ones to use with which wax type. There are many books on the subject and there is a lot of information available on line at the various candle-making supply websites. Wicks also come in many different sizes and they have numbers assigned to them. It is important that you learn what these numbers mean to help you decide which types of wicks to purchase.

You will also need to determine what diameter your candle will be as this will also play an important part in the type of wick you will need. Usually, the larger diameter candle you are making, the larger wick size you will need.

In particular, if you are making container candles, you need to be sure that the wick is big enough to melt the wax completely across the top of the candle. You do not want your candle to burn with a small hole down the center. This is called "tunneling". When this happens, the wick burns the hole down the center and you are left with a tunnel of wax around the sides of the container which does not burn.

You do not want to use a wick that is too big for the

candle you are making as this will cause the candle to burn too fast and will cause excessive smoking and soot.

In summary, there are many different factors that will determine which wicks will be best for your particular candles. You certainly can and should get recommendations from manufacturers but you also will probably need to do some type of experimentation to see what really works for your particular candles and just what type of wicks you prefer to use.

How to Choose a Candle Wick

So, you have decided that you would like to start making your own candles. There are different types of wicks you can choose from, depending on the type of candle you are making. From the type of wax used the amount of dye, fragrance, and how big the candle container will be. The longevity of your candle can depend on the type of wick chosen. There are several variables that will affect the outcome of your candle; so choosing the appropriate one is important.

There are some problems that can happen with wicks, such as mushrooming. This can occur when the wax in a candle burns faster than the wick, which can cause a blackened bit of excess that could result in a burnt black ball hanging over the candle.

Chapter 10 : Making Your Own Wicks

There are some common wicks chosen to be used in the candle making process.

An ECO wick flat wick braided with interwoven paper threads. These wicks are known to work well with paraffin and natural waxes. They are solid scented, colored, pillar and container candles and have been found to perform very well in paraffin and natural wax blends. When wicking, these are ideal for tea lights and votives.

HTP (High Temperature Paper) this is more of a universal wick. It tends to work well for paraffin, gel and vegetable waxes that often require hotter burning applications as well as minimize carbon build-up.

Wooden wicks are used with sox container wax and can burn up to about ten hours. They are the newest type of wicking that is being used today. It is important to make sure that these wicks are treated, because untreated wicks sometimes don't light, or only stay lit for a short period of time. These also have that crackling wood fire sound while wood wick burning. This wicking method works really well for containers, pillars, and votives.

Zinc core wicks are also another type commonly used. This type tends to be easier to stay standing straight and centered while the candle burning.

Untabbed wicks are used for pillar candles. It is self-trimming, which helps reduce carbon buildup.

Once you have chosen the wick that best fits your needs, you will need to make sure you have a tab (also known as wick bases) especially if you will be making votive or container candles, since it will help your wick stand up straight. You will need to make sure you pick a base that is the appropriate size for your candle.

Having a good idea about some of the wicks that are available to choose from, will make it easier for you to narrow it down to the type you will need, based on the type of candle you will be creating. If you want to test out different wicks, you can often find sample packs that will allow you to choose the perfect wick!

What's the Best Type of Candle?

Once upon a time candles were a necessity. If the sun went down and you wanted to be able to see, you better have a stack of candles sitting around and ready to go.

These days, candles are more of something to appreciate than a necessity. This has led to candles not being just one, uniform style, to create a particular function, but instead to their being created in a variety of styles, colours, designs and scents to fit any mood or theme. As you consider the right kinds of candles to bring into your home, start by looking at the shape:

Pillar Soy Candles

Chapter 10 : Making Your Own Wicks

In days of old when candles were being used as a way to light a path at night, generally these types of candles were put to work. They are medium to tall in height and thick enough to give off a long burn, lighting the way through a long night.

In today's world, these are often the centrepiece candles for a candle arrangement as they can stand up above flowers or other decorations.

Votive Soy Candles

If you have a little candle holder or decorative candle bowl that you want to make shine, you may want to pick up a few votive soy candles. These are shorter than pillars and usually about 1 ½ - 2 inches wide.

Jar Soy Candles

By far the most popular of candle designs are jar soy candles. The reason for this is that not only do these candles give off a beautiful glow, but they also come in their own decorative container, as they are moulded directly in a jar.

These are also thought of as the safest of candle designs by many since they are self-contained and you can put a lid back on top after you have used them, avoiding any smouldering or hot wax issues.

Speciality Soy Candles

While the above candles are traditional designs, some people want more than traditional designs. For these people there are a number of speciality soy candles out there. From candles that look like teddy bears to those that take on the shape of a famous sculpture, there are plenty of speciality soy candles on the market that are as much decoration by their shape as for being a candle.

Scented or Unscented

Once you have selected a shape for your soy candles, there is still another consideration to make. Do you want them to be scented or unscented candles?

Scented

One of the things many people love most about candles is the scents that come from them. The use of essential oils will allow candles to give off scents as they burn. There are a number of scents on the market these days from floral bouquets that can make you thing spring has sprung to apple, gingerbread and cinnamon that make you feel like you have been whisked back to your childhood holiday gatherings.

Unscented

If you are using your soy candles as merely display pieces to complete a centrepiece on a table or to light up a bowl, vase or other arrangement, you may not want the candles to give off scents. In this case you may choose unscented candles.

Making a Selection

Selecting candles is a very personal thing for most people. Take your time. The candles aren't going anywhere. Enjoy the process of looking through all the colours, shapes and scents until you find the combination that is best for you.

CHAPTER ELEVEN

Step by Step Melting Wax Candle Making

Making Candles is a great hobby for beginners and can become profitable. With a little creativity you can make some beautiful gifts. The most important rule of melting wax candles is safety, be sure that children and animals are kept out of the candle making area, candle wax is extremely flammable and will catch fire at 375 degrees F, it should never be heated to the point where it begins to boil or smoke. Follow steps 1 through 5 and you will be on your way to some homemade wax candles.

Choose a mold:

Your mold needs to be something smooth and easy for you to pull the candle out after it has dried. You can oil the inside of the mold with vegetable oil for easy removal.

Set a double boiler:

Get a medium sized can or pot and place it in a second larger pot. Fill the larger pot with a couple inches of water and heat on high, and begin candles.

Chapter 10 : Step by Step Melting Wax Candle Making

Melting wax candles:

You can either use paraffin or leftover wax from old candles (If your using old candles make sure you remove any old burnt wick). Break the wax into chunks and place it in your double boiler, make sure you are constantly string it until the candle wax melted. If you would like to add color to your candle, you can get small pieces of crayons and mix them into your melting wax candles. You can also decide if you would like to scent your candle with either fragrance oil or perfume. Your candle is on its way!

Making your wicks:

Cut a piece of string that is double the length of you candle mold. Dip the string in your melted wax and let it hang from something and dry out so that when your mold is ready you will have nice straight wicks.

Pouring your wax candles:

Get your mold ready; and being very careful while using oven mitts, poor your melting wax candles into the mold. Place your wick in the center of the mold using a pencil to suspend it and keep it centered. Let your candle cool down and dry for about a day, you may think its ready earlier but the center can still be very soft. After your candle is cooled down completely, carefully remove the candle and then the best step. Enjoy your new homemade designed candles!

Basic Component of Any Candle

Regardless whether you are hobby candle maker or making candles is your business, you need wax. Candle making wax is the basic component of any candle. I'm not using the word "the most important" component, because candle without the wick is only a nice waxy sculpture.

There are several types of candle making waxes available on the market, and which one you are going to use is entirely up to you. As you progress and become more and more confident with making candles, I'm sure you will want to experiment with most of them. Your choice of wax will also depend on type of a candle you want to make and the effect you want to achieve.

- The candle making wax I like the most is the beeswax. The reason for that could be my sentimental connection and the soft spot for the beekeeping. Beeswax is one of the natural types of wax and it comes from the renewable source. Bees produce wax in order to build their honeycombs and to seal off the individual cells filled with pollen, propolis and nectar. In the bee colony, honeycomb also hosts larvae as well as bee queen. When working with beeswax, never melt it on the direct source of the heat. Always use double boiler because the beeswax is a flammable substance. Melting point is at about 64 degrees Celsius (147 degrees F). The chemical structure of the beeswax is going to be damages if you overheat it. The color of natural beeswax varies from the white to yellow, depending on the pollen and propolis deposits.

- Palm wax is another type of natural candle making wax. It comes from palm oil production countries - Malaysia and Indonesia. Palm wax a non-edible product which burns longer then paraffin.

- Natural type of wax with fast growing popularity is soy wax. It is easier to work with than with paraffin. Also, it comes in the flake form which makes it easier to measure desired quantity. Price wise, it is much more affordable than beeswax. Cleaning up of any spills when working with soy wax is simple - just use warm soapy water. Soy wax is produced by hydrogenation of soy bean oil. Soy bean is grown in Asia as well as in USA, Brazil and Argentina.

- Bayberry wax is the outer coat of some varieties of the bayberry fruits. This type of natural wax is used to produce candles. Apart from Australasia, bayberry bush is growing widely around the world

- Gel wax is a clear, jelly like substance. Depending on the density, it comes as: low, medium or high density gel wax. Which density to use is going to be important for you when you decide to introduce the fragrance to your gel wax candles. The denser the gel wax, the more fragrance it can hold. When creating gel wax candle, bear in mind that you will have to use container to house the gel wax. Also, when melting gel wax, you must be aware that this type of wax will become syrupy (not thinner!) when exposed to the higher temperatures.

- Paraffin wax is probably the most widely used type of wax in the candle making world. Because of its low cost, it is makes a good choice to begin your candle making venture with paraffin. Paraffin is also often mixed with some other types of wax for variety of reasons. Paraffin becomes flammable substance if overheated...just like any other types of wax.

It doesn't really matter which candle making wax you'll choose to begin your candle carrier with. Try to work with all types of wax...it is like a trying out a new recipe. Basic candle making principals are similar, but every type of candle wax will bring a new "flavour" to your experience.

Making Gel Candles for Fun & Profit

There are a few items you will need to gather before you can start making your gel candles. The most basic are supply containers, gels, pans, wicks, and of course, your kitchen range. Below is a detailed list of the items you will need, and most of these items are available at your local craft and variety stores.

Containers:

It's best to use a heat resistant glass, but there are also many types of glass and acrylics.

Materials:

Gel Wax, Paraffin when specified in a recipe, candle scent, candle dye, wick, wick clip, and wick base.

Supplies:

Craft sticks, knife, spoon, candy thermometer, pliers, small sauce pan, double boiler for paraffin when used, cooking oil spray, non-stick cookie sheet, ice cream scoop, ice pick, Potato peeler for the dye, stove burner, small deep metal pans, and molds.

Wicks & Clips:

Use large bleached wicks. Gel candles burn longer than paraffin candles so a large wick is required for the additional burn time. Do not use wire wicks these will leave debris in the gel. Use a metal base clip and crimp it to one end of the wick with pliers or use a small washer.

Dyes & Scents:

Candles dyes are great to use because their color is translucent. Crayons can also be used if the proper dyes are not available at your local stores. Candle dyes come in different forms, from wax squares, to liquids and powders. You can mix colors to form additional colors. Scents are fun to add to make the candle fragrant. Scents come in the form of oil based liquids, pellets and wax solids. You add scent before pouring the candle this avoids evaporation.

Additives & Release Agents:

If using paraffin, add stearic acid to increase the hardness and raise the melting point. Use spray cooking oil or silicone spray to aid in the release of the molds.

Submerged Objects:

In order to submerge objects in your gel candles they must be resistant to burning and melting. Items that work well are buttons, marbles, toys and jewels. Do not use highly flammable items. Some objects will float so you may have to add the items as the gel cools and thickens. This is where the craft sticks or knife comes in handy. You can push items down that float to the top.

Heating Wax:

Paraffin should be heated to 130 degrees F to 140 degrees F. The melting point of gel wax is between 160 degrees and 170 degrees F. If you are melting Paraffin you should always use a double boiler. Gel wax can be heated directly on the burner set at a medium to low heat. Tip: Tear gel into small pieces to control the amount of bubbles.

CAUTION:

Always be careful when melting wax. It is highly flammable. Make sure your area is well ventilated. Never leave unattended or around young children without supervision.

Clean Up:

Use dish soap and hot water to clean utensils, counter tops and tools. Run paraffin under hot water then under soapy water. You can scrape wax off counter tops, or use small amounts of turpentine to aid in removal (be sure to test first).

CONCLUSION

The most important aspect in candle making is the test-run. If the candles are to be used personally, a test run may not be necessary. However, if the intention is to sell it, then market testing is needed. There is need to test the products with friends and neighbors and ask to get feedback from them. Comments should be made by them as regards the color, scent, look, and pricing before you offer the products for sale.

DISCLAIMER

Disclaimer All the material contained in this book is provided for educational and informational purposes only. No responsibility can be taken for any results or outcomes resulting from the use

of this material. While every attempt has been made to provide information that is both accurate and effective, the author does not assume any responsibility for the accuracy or use/misuse of this information.

Printed in Great Britain
by Amazon